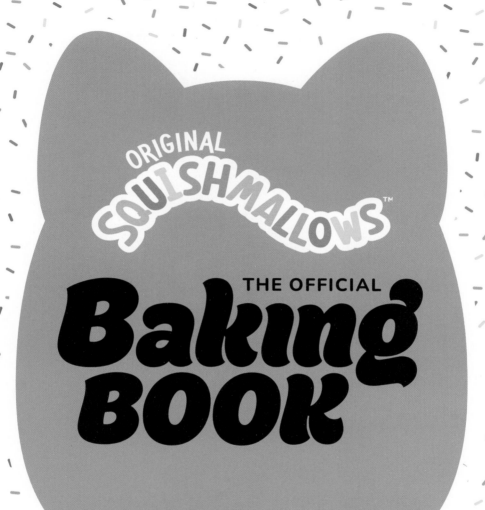

ORIGINAL
SQUISHMALLOWS™

THE OFFICIAL
Baking
BOOK

WHITE LION
PUBLISHING

Contents

Introduction

Welcome to the Original Squishmallows baking book, a delightful adventure into the adorable world of these cuddly 'Mallows!

The culinary journey within these pages takes you through a range of bakes both big and small, including treats suitable for a variety of holidays and celebrations. Each recipe is crafted with love and a sprinkle of squishy magic. You'll discover even more about each of your favourite 'Mallow friends through these 'Mallowlicious inspired receipes. From beautifully decorated cakes to cookies bursting with flavour, each recipe is crafted to bring a smile to your face and warmth to your heart.

Along with the bakes, you'll find a selection of delicious drink recipes. We've covered hot and cold, refreshing, comforting and thirst-quenching, so there's something here for everyone. And combining the bakes and drinks – think banana bread with pumpkin-spice latte; two-tone cupcakes with watermelon fresca; gingerbread houses with hot cocoa – will make for a feast that's truly flavoursome and memorable.

With creativity, colour, and a sprinkle of magic, the recipes capture the essence of these lovable plush companions, giving you a range of treats you can make and dive into in cosy kitchens, on magical picnics and at dreamy tea parties.

Your invitation to bake with the Squishmallows awaits. Enjoy every scrumptious moment!

Bakes

Ryan's meringue sandwiches

Meet Ryan, he's not your average husky. He loves strawberry season almost as much as he loves to spend time learning about robots and technology. One day, he hopes to be a famous inventor – his first invention might be an instant strawberry dessert!

Makes about 12 sandwiches

For the meringues
225g (8oz/1⅛ cups) caster
    (superfine) sugar
100g (3½oz) egg whites
    (from about 3 large eggs)
a pinch of salt
red food colouring paste

For the filling
200g (7oz) strawberries
400ml (13½fl oz/1⅔ cups)
    double (heavy) cream
1 tsp vanilla extract or
    vanilla bean paste

1 Preheat the oven to (fan) 80°C/100°C/200°F/gas ½.

2 Combine the sugar and egg whites in the bowl of a stand mixer, add the salt and place over a pan of barely simmering water – do not allow the bottom of the bowl to touch the water. Mix with a balloon whisk for about 5 minutes, until the sugar has completely dissolved and the mixture starts to turn white and thicken.

3 Working quickly, remove the bowl from the heat and whisk in the stand mixer fitted with the whisk attachment on medium–high speed for about 5 minutes until the meringue is very stiff, white and cold.

4 Using a clean craft brush, paint three stripes of red food colouring paste on the inside of piping bag, going from the nozzle towards the opening, evenly spaced apart. Carefully fill the bag with the meringue mixture. Pipe the meringue into 5–6cm (2–2½in)-wide discs on the lined baking sheets – the mixture should make about 24 meringue discs.

5 Bake in the middle of the oven for 1 hour until crisp. Turn the oven off and leave the meringues to cool inside.

continued overleaf

Ryan's meringue sandwiches
continued

You will need:
stand mixer
clean craft brush
1 large disposable piping
  (pastry) bag fitted with a
  medium open-star nozzle
2 large baking sheets lined
  with baking paper or
  silicone baking mats
hand-held electric whisk
  or balloon whisk

6 To make the filling, remove the green leafy tops from the strawberries and roughly chop the fruit. Whip the cream with the vanilla using a hand-held electric whisk or balloon whisk until it holds soft floppy peaks. Add the chopped strawberries and fold in using a large metal spoon or rubber spatula.

7 Turn half of the meringues over so that they are flat side uppermost. Top with a tablespoon of strawberry-cream filling and sandwich with the remaining meringues. Serve immediately.

STORAGE: Meringues will keep unfilled in an airtight box at room temperature for 3–4 days. Once filled, serve immediately.

Claudia's Key lime pies

Claudia wakes up with the sunrise! She's a responsible little beet and supports all her friends and family with anything they need – even if it's just for a laugh. Claudia knows that generosity comes in all forms, including goofy ones. And nobody makes a better Key lime pie!

Makes 6 pies

For the base
250g (9oz) digestive biscuits (or Graham crackers)
85g (3oz) unsalted butter
1 tbsp cocoa powder

For the filling
4 large limes
3 medium egg yolks
1 x 397g (14oz) tin/can condensed milk

To decorate
25g (1oz) dark (bittersweet) chocolate, melted
150ml (5fl oz/⅔ cup) double (heavy) cream
1 lime

You will need:
food processor or rolling pin
6 x 8cm (3in) individual tart rings or loose-bottomed tart tins with a depth of 3cm (1¼in)
baking tray lined with baking paper
1 small piping (pastry) bag with a small star nozzle
ballon whisk

STORAGE: The pies will keep in an airtight box in the fridge for up to 2 days.

1 Preheat the oven to (fan) 150°C/170°C/325°F/gas mark 3.

2 Crush the biscuits to a sandy texture either in a freezer bag, using a rolling pin to bash them, or in a food processor, then tip them into a mixing bowl. Melt the butter, add it to the biscuit crumbs along with the cocoa powder and mix well to thoroughly combine.

3 Arrange the tart rings or tins on the lined baking tray and divide the crumbs between the rings, pressing them down to evenly line the base and sides of each. Bake in the oven for 8–10 minutes until dry.

4 Meanwhile, prepare the filling. Finely grate the zest from the limes and tip into a mixing bowl. Add the egg yolks and mix with a balloon whisk for 1 minute until combined and the egg yolks are paler in colour. Add the condensed milk and whisk again until thoroughly combined. Squeeze the juice from the limes – you will need about 120ml (4fl oz/½ cup) – add to the mixture and beat until smooth.

5 Divide the mixture evenly among the biscuit bases, spread to level out and return to the oven for 8–10 minutes, until the filling has just set. Remove from the oven and leave to cool, then chill for 2 hours or until ready to serve.

6 Remove the pies from the rings or tins and place on serving plates.

7 Drizzle the melted chocolate over the top of each pie. Whisk the cream in a bowl until it just holds firm peaks, spoon into the piping (pastry) bag and pipe the cream decoratively on top of each pie. Cut the lime into thin slices and arrange on top to serve.

Bethany's Linzer love heart cookies

Bethany's favorite meal is breakfast, especially fresh biscuits and jam! Her mom makes them every Friday. On the weekend Bethany helps her mom in the garden, tending to all the yummy berries she uses for jam.

Makes about 24 sandwiched cookies

225g (8oz) unsalted butter, softened

100g (3½oz/½ cup) caster (superfine) sugar

50g (1¾oz/scant ½ cup) icing (powdered) sugar, plus extra for dusting

3 medium egg yolks

1 tsp vanilla extract or vanilla bean paste

1 tsp finely grated lemon zest (from an unwaxed lemon)

275g (9¾oz/generous 2 cups) plain (all-purpose) flour, plus extra for dusting

½ tsp baking powder

a pinch of salt

1 Beat the butter and both sugars together in the bowl of a stand mixer fitted with the creamer attachment until pale, light and fluffy. Scrape down the sides of the bowl using a rubber spatula, then add the egg yolks one at a time, mixing between each one. Add the vanilla and lemon zest and mix again until combined.

2 Sift the flour, baking powder and salt into the bowl, add the ground almonds (almond meal) and slowly mix into the creamed mixture until smooth. Flatten the dough into a disc, wrap in cling film (plastic wrap) and chill for at least 1 hour or until firm.

3 Lightly dust the work surface with flour, unwrap the dough and roll it out to a thickness of around 3mm (⅛in). Stamp out 48 cookies using the fluted round cookie cutter. Reshape any leftover dough into a ball, re-roll and cut out more cookies. Arrange the cookies on the lined baking sheets and chill for 20 minutes.

4 Preheat the oven to (fan) 150°C/170°C/325°F/gas mark 3.

5 Using the heart cutter, stamp out shapes from the middle of one half of the cookies.

continued overleaf

Bethany's Linzer love-heart cookies *continued*

75g (2¾oz) ground almonds (almond meal)
4–5 tbsp good-quality raspberry jam

You will need:
stand mixer
5cm (2in) fluted round cookie cutter
2cm (¾in) heart cutter
2 large baking sheets lined with baking paper

STORAGE: The biscuits will keep in an airtight box for up to 4 days.

6 Bake the biscuits in batches on the middle shelf of the oven for 12–14 minutes or until pale golden brown. Remove from the oven and leave to cool on the baking sheets for 2 minutes, then carefully transfer to a wire rack.

7 Once the biscuits are completely cold, spread a teaspoon of jam onto the solid biscuits, leaving a 1cm (½in) border all around the edge. Dust the heart biscuits with icing sugar, press on top of each jam-covered biscuit and serve.

TIP: Use apricot jam in place of raspberry, or for a more colourful and flavourful spread use 3 different types of jams to fill the cut-outs.

Tatiana's blueberry cheesecake

Tatiana loves dancing, baking, and exploring with her friends. She wants to save the world one day at a time. Catch Tatiana with her friends out in the wild or in the library reading up on her next big adventure!

Makes 1 large cheesecake (serves 8–10)

175g (6¼oz) digestive biscuits (or Graham crackers)
65g (2oz) unsalted butter
600g (1lb 5oz/ 2½ cups) full-fat cream cheese
125g (4½oz/generous ½ cup) soured cream
150g (5½oz/¾ cup) caster (superfine) sugar
2 tbsp cornflour (cornstarch)
grated zest and juice of ½ unwaxed lemon
2 tsp vanilla extract or vanilla bean paste
3 medium eggs, lightly beaten
225g (8oz) blueberries

1 Preheat the oven to (fan) 150°C/170°C/325°F/gas mark 3.

2 Finely crush the biscuits either in a freezer bag, using a rolling pin to bash them, or in a food processor, then tip the crumbs into a bowl. Melt the butter and mix into the crumbs. Tip into the prepared tin and press into an even layer over the base. Bake on the middle shelf of the oven for 5 minutes until crisp.

3 Combine the cream cheese, soured cream, caster sugar and cornflour in a mixing bowl and beat until smooth and thoroughly combined. Add the lemon zest, lemon juice and vanilla. Mix again until smooth. Add the beaten eggs and beat again until the mixture is thoroughly combined.

4 Fold the blueberries into the mixture, carefully pour the filling onto the base and spread it level. Wrap the outside of the tin in a double thickness of foil and place the tin on a baking tray.

5 Bake on the middle shelf of the oven for 35–40 minutes or until just set. Turn the oven off and leave the cheesecake inside for 15 minutes with the door closed, then open the oven door slightly and leave the cheesecake inside for a further 5 minutes.

6 Remove the cheesecake from the oven and leave to cool completely before covering and chilling.

continued overleaf

Tatiana's blueberry cheesecake
continued

For the blueberry compote
300g (10½oz) blueberries
100g (3½oz/½ cup) caster
(superfine) sugar
juice of ½ lemon
2 tsp cornflour (cornstarch)

You will need:
rolling pin or food processor
20cm (8in) round springform
cake tin, greased and base
lined with baking paper
baking tray

7 To make the blueberry compote, tip half of the blueberries into a saucepan with the sugar and lemon juice and cook over a low–medium heat for 4–5 minutes, until the berries have started to soften and release their juice. Add the remaining berries and cook for a moment longer to soften them slightly. Mix the cornflour with 2 teaspoons of water in a small bowl, add to the blueberry mixture and cook for a minute more, stirring constantly to thicken slightly.

8 Remove from the heat, tip into a bowl and leave until cold.

9 Carefully remove the cheesecake from the tin and place on a serving plate. Top with the blueberry compote to serve.

STORAGE: You can store the cheesecake in an airtight box in the fridge for up to 2 days.

Chanel's two-tone cupcakes

Meet Chanel. She's sweeter than your average pastry and she's a pastry chef who loves giving back! In her spare time, Chanel likes to volunteer at the local food pantry and teaches cake baking and decorating classes.

Makes 12 cupcakes

125g (4½oz) unsalted butter, softened

125g (4½oz/⅔ cup) caster (superfine) sugar

2 medium eggs, lightly beaten

1 tsp vanilla extract or vanilla bean paste

1 tsp finely grated lemon zest (from an unwaxed lemon)

125g (4½oz/1 cup) plain (all-purpose) flour

1½ tsp baking powder

a pinch of salt

2 tbsp soured cream

edible sugar sprinkles, to serve

1 Preheat the oven to (fan) 160°C/180°C/350°F/gas mark 4.

2 Cream the butter and sugar together in a stand mixer fitted with the creamer attachment for about 3 minutes until really pale, light and fluffy. Gradually add the beaten eggs, mixing well between each addition and scraping down the sides of the bowl with a rubber spatula from time to time. Add the vanilla and the lemon zest and mix again.

3 Sift the flour, baking powder and salt into the bowl, add the soured cream and mix again on slow speed until fully combined.

4 Divide the mixture evenly between the paper cases and bake on the middle shelf of the oven for about 20 minutes, until the cakes are golden, well risen and a skewer inserted into the middle of the cakes comes out clean.

5 Remove from the oven and allow the cakes to rest in the tin for 3–4 minutes, then transfer to a wire rack until completely cold.

6 Meanwhile make the meringue buttercream following the recipe on page 128.

continued overleaf

Chanel's two-tone cupcakes
continued

For the meringue buttercream
1 quantity of meringue
   buttercream
   (see page 128)
pink and green food
   colouring pastes

You will need:
stand mixer
12-hole muffin tin lined
   with paper cases
large piping (pastry) bag
   with medium star nozzle

7 Divide the buttercream between three bowls and use food colouring paste to tint two of the bowlfuls in contrasting colours and leave the third bowl white.

8 Open the piping bag wide and spoon the buttercreams neatly each into one third of the bag to fill. Twist the end to seal and pipe a generous swirl of marbled buttercream on top of each cupcake. Scatter with sprinkles to serve.

STORAGE: The cupcakes will keep in an airtight box for up to 3 days.

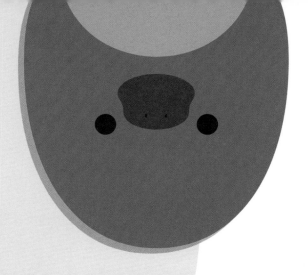

Santino's blueberry pancakes

Santino makes the best blueberry pancakes, his dad taught him how to add the blueberries just right. When he's not making pancakes for all his friends, you can find Santino playing soccer – he wants to be a professional goalie someday.

Makes about 15 pancakes

For the blueberry compote
200g (7oz) blueberries
25g (1oz/2 tbsp) caster (superfine) sugar
juice of ½ lemon

For the pancakes
175g (6¼oz/1½ cups) plain (all-purpose) flour
15g (½oz/1¼ tbsp) caster (superfine) sugar
½ tsp baking powder
½ tsp bicarbonate of soda (baking soda)
a pinch of salt
250ml (8½fl oz/1 cup) buttermilk
2 tsp vanilla extract or vanilla bean paste
1 medium egg
20g (¾oz) unsalted butter, melted, plus extra for cooking
125g (4½oz) blueberries
maple syrup, to serve

1 Start by making the blueberry compote. Put the blueberries, sugar and lemon juice in a small saucepan and place over a low–medium heat. Cook for 4–5 minutes, stirring often, until the blueberries just soften and start to become juicy. Remove from the heat and set aside until ready to serve.

2 To make the pancakes, sift the flour, sugar, baking powder, bicarbonate of soda and salt into a mixing bowl. In a jug combine the buttermilk, vanilla and egg and mix to combine.

3 Pour the buttermilk mixture into the dry ingredients, add the melted butter and mix with a balloon whisk until combined.

4 Heat a large frying pan (skillet) over a low–medium heat. Add a little butter and spoon tablespoons of pancake mix into the pan – depending on the size of your pan you may be able to cook 3 or 4 pancakes at one time. Cook for about 2 minutes, until bubbles start to appear on the top of the pancakes. Scatter 3 or 4 blueberries onto each pancake and, using a fish slice or palette knife, carefully flip the pancakes over and cook the underside for a further minute until golden and puffy.

5 Remove from the pan and keep warm while you cook the remaining pancakes, adding more butter to the frying pan for each batch.

6 Serve the pancakes with the warm blueberry compote and plenty of maple syrup drizzled over the top.

STORAGE: Best eaten immediately.

Sunny's honey buns

Need to know if it's going to be raining next week or if you should pack a jacket? Ask Sunny! She's always had a knack for knowing just what's going to happen next when it comes to the weather. Sunny looks forward to becoming a weather reporter when she's older.

Makes 12 buns

450g (1lb/3¾ cups) strong white bread flour, plus extra for dusting
2 tbsp dried milk powder
7g (¼oz/1¾ tsp) fast-action dried yeast
1 tsp salt
150ml (5fl oz/⅔ cup) whole (full-fat) milk, warmed
50g (1¾oz) runny honey
2 medium eggs, lightly beaten
100g (3½oz) unsalted butter, softened
1 tsp vanilla extract

For the filling
150g (5½oz/¾ cup) caster (superfine) sugar
125g (4½oz) unsalted butter, softened
3 tbsp runny honey
½ tsp ground cinnamon
1 tsp vanilla extract

You will need:
stand mixer
piping (pastry) bag
ruler
pizza wheel
2 baking sheets lined with baking paper

1 Tip the flour into the bowl of a stand mixer, add the milk powder, yeast and salt and mix to combine using a balloon whisk. Make a well in the middle of the dry ingredients, add the warm milk, honey, eggs, butter and vanilla and mix on slow speed until combined.

2 Scrape down the sides of the bowl and continue mixing for 7–8 minutes until the dough is silky smooth and elastic. Shape the dough into a ball, lightly oil the mixing bowl, return the dough to the bowl, cover and leave at room temperature for about 1½ hours until the dough has risen and doubled in size.

3 Meanwhile, prepare the filling. Combine all the ingredients in a bowl and mix until smooth. Spoon into a piping bag and set aside.

4 Dust the work surface with flour, turn the dough out of the bowl and pat into a rectangle. Slowly roll the dough into a neat 40 x 40cm (16 x 16in) square, lightly flouring the work surface and rolling pin as needed.

5 Trim all four sides of the dough square to neaten and, using a ruler and pizza wheel, cut the dough into twelve 3cm (1¼in)-thick vertical strips. Pipe the filling in a neat line down the length of each strip. Taking one strip at a time, roll the strip away from you into a neat spiral. Tuck the end underneath and place on one of the lined baking sheets. Repeat to make 12 buns.

6 Loosely cover with oiled cling film (plastic wrap) and leave to rise at room temperature for about 45 minutes until doubled in size.

7 Preheat the oven to (fan) 160°C/180°C/350°F/gas mark 4.

8 Remove the cling film and bake the buns on the middle shelf of the oven for 25 minutes until well risen and golden brown.

STORAGE: Best eaten on the day of making, but can be stored somewhere cool in an airtight box for up to 2 days.

Lesedi's cinnamon rolls

Do you know any owls obsessed with cinnamon? It's time to meet Lesedi, the cinnamon queen! She loves cinnamon rolls, cinnamon hot chocolate, and even cinnamon lip gloss! When she grows up, maybe she'll start her own cinnamon restaurant, would you eat there?

Makes 12 buns

500g (1lb 2oz/4 cups) strong white bread flour, plus extra for dusting

50g (1¾oz/¼ cup) caster (superfine) sugar

7g (¼oz/1¾ tsp) fast-action dried yeast

a large pinch of salt

200ml (7fl oz/generous ¾ cup) whole (full-fat) milk

100g (3½oz) unsalted butter, softened

2 medium eggs, beaten

For the cinnamon filling

125g (4½oz) unsalted butter, softened

100g (3½oz/generous ½ cup) soft light brown sugar

4 tsp ground cinnamon

1 Combine the flour, sugar, yeast and salt in the bowl of a stand mixer fitted with a dough hook. Warm the milk until it's tepid (too hot and it will kill the yeast) and add to the bowl along with the butter and beaten eggs. Mix on slow speed until combined, then increase the speed to medium and continue kneading for 6–8 minutes until the dough is smooth and elastic.

2 Shape the dough into a ball, place it back in the bowl, cover and leave at room temperature for 1–1½ hours or until doubled in size.

3 To make the cinnamon filling, beat the butter with the brown sugar and cinnamon in a bowl until smooth and creamy.

4 Lightly flour a work surface, turn the dough out onto the surface and knead it lightly for 10 seconds. Roll the dough into a neat square about 1cm (½in) thick and measuring about 40 x 40cm (16 x 16in). Spread the cinnamon filling over the dough, leaving a border of about 5mm (¼in) around the edges.

5 Roll the dough up into a neat spiral roll, starting with the side closest to you and keeping the roll even and firm. Transfer the roll to a lined baking sheet and chill for 10 minutes – this will make cutting easier.

continued overleaf

Lesedi's cinnamon rolls *continued*

For the cream cheese frosting

125g (4½oz) unsalted butter, softened
125g (4½oz/½ cup) cream cheese, at room temperature
1 tsp vanilla extract or vanilla bean paste
150g (5½oz/1¼ cups) icing (powdered) sugar, sifted

You will need:

stand mixer
lined baking sheet
1 deep 23 x 33cm (9 x 13in) baking tin, base and sides lined with baking paper

STORAGE: Best eaten on the day of making, but can be stored in an airtight box somewhere cool for up to 2 days.

6 Using a sharp knife, trim the ends of the roll then cut into 12 even slices. Place cut side uppermost in the lined baking tin. Cover loosely and leave at room temperature for about 45 minutes to prove and nearly double in size again.

7 Meanwhile preheat the oven to (fan) 160°C/180°C/350°F/gas mark 4.

8 Bake the buns in the oven for 25 minutes until golden brown and well risen.

9 While the buns are baking, prepare the cream cheese frosting. Using a wooden spoon or rubber spatula, cream the butter in a bowl until soft and light. Add the cream cheese and vanilla and beat again to combine. Add the icing sugar and mix until smooth and creamy.

10 Once baked, leave the buns to cool in the tin for 5–10 minutes then spread with half of the frosting. Leave until cold then spread with the remaining frosting to serve.

TIP: You can also make these buns in a 12-hole muffin tin if preferred. Grease the muffin tin well before filling.

Edie's Easter egg fridge cake

Have you heard the weekly weather report? Make sure you tune in to Edie's Eggcellent Weather Report to find out. Easter egg Edie loves to talk about the weather, and always tries to dress the part. Her favorite ensemble is a jumpsuit with lightning bolts that glow in the dark.

Makes about 25 squares

100g (3½oz) milk chocolate, chopped
200g (7oz) dark (bittersweet) chocolate, chopped
125g (4½oz) unsalted butter, diced
125g (4½oz/½ cup) golden syrup (light treacle)
300g (10½oz) digestive biscuits (or Graham crackers)
150g (5½oz) crisp-coated mini eggs
75g (2¾oz) glacé cherries
50g (1¾oz) pecans
75g (2¾oz) mini marshmallows
50g (1¾oz) raisins

To decorate

75g (2¾oz) milk chocolate
75g (2¾oz) dark (bittersweet) chocolate
100g (3½oz) white chocolate
150g (5½oz) crisp-coated mini eggs
3 tbsp colourful edible sprinkles

You will need:

20 x 30cm (8 x 12in) brownie tin, base and sides lined with baking paper

1 Tip the milk and dark chocolate into a large heatproof bowl. Add the butter and golden syrup and melt either over a pan of simmering water (being careful to ensure the bottom of the bowl isn't touching the water) or in the microwave on a low setting, stirring from time to time. Remove from the heat and leave to cool.

2 Break the biscuits into roughly 1cm (½in) pieces. Roughly chop the mini eggs, glacé cherries and pecans, add to the biscuit pieces with the mini marshmallows and raisins and mix to combine.

3 Pour over the melted chocolate mixture and mix to thoroughly combine. Spoon into the prepared tin and spread level using the back of a spoon. Cover the surface with a sheet of baking paper and press the surface flat. Chill for about 1 hour or until set.

4 For the topping, melt the milk, dark and white chocolate in separate bowls. Stir until smooth and leave to cool slightly. Using a teaspoon, drop random dollops of milk chocolate over the top of the fridge cake and do the same with the dark and white chocolate, filling in the gaps. Gently shake the tin to level the melted chocolate and use a wooden skewer to marble the chocolates together.

5 Scatter the top of the melted chocolate with the mini eggs and sprinkles and chill for about 30 minutes or until the chocolate has set, then use the lining paper to lift the fridge cake out of the tin and cut into about 25 squares or bars to serve.

STORAGE: Will keep for up to 4 days in an airtight box.

Satine's carrot cake

Satine is a total brunch bunny! She orders way too much food and packs whatever is left over to save for later. Satine hangs out all morning with orange juice and coffee, either reading the morning paper or chatting with a buddy. Join Satine and don't forget to bring your appetite!

Makes 1 large cake (serves 10)

For the marzipan carrots
100g (3½oz) marzipan
orange food colouring paste
3 rosemary sprigs or
   2 angelica sticks

For the cake
250g (9oz) coarsely grated
   carrots (grated weight)
grated zest and juice of
   1 orange
30g (1¼oz) desiccated
   coconut
1 ripe banana, peeled
   and mashed
50g (1¾oz) pecans,
   roughly chopped
3 medium eggs
250ml (8½fl oz/1 cup)
   sunflower oil
250g (9oz/1¼ cups) golden
   caster (superfine) sugar
2 tbsp whole (full-fat) milk
1 tsp vanilla extract or
   vanilla bean paste

1 Start by making the marzipan carrots, which will need to dry for at least 3 hours or overnight. Tint the marzipan orange using orange food colouring paste. Break off 1 teaspoon of the marzipan and roll it between your hands into a carrot shape, place on a sheet of baking paper and repeat with the remaining marzipan. Use a skewer or cocktail stick to make a small hole in the top of each carrot. Leave the carrots uncovered at room temperature to dry for at least 3 hours or overnight.

2 Preheat the oven to (fan) 170°C/190°C/375°F/gas mark 5.

3 In a large mixing bowl, combine the grated carrots, orange zest and juice, desiccated coconut, mashed banana and chopped pecans.

4 In another bowl, whisk the eggs, oil, sugar, milk and vanilla until smooth. Add the carrot mixture and mix well. Sift the flour, baking powder, bicarbonate of soda, ground cinnamon and salt into the bowl and fold in using a large spoon or rubber spatula until thoroughly combined.

5 Divide the mixture evenly between the prepared tins, spread to level out and bake on the middle shelf of the oven for 25–30 minutes or until a skewer inserted into the middle of each cake comes out clean.

6 Cool the cakes in the tins for 10 minutes before turning out onto a wire rack. Turn the cakes the right way up and leave to cool completely.

7 To make the frosting, beat the butter in a bowl until pale and light, add the cream cheese and mix again until smooth. Add the icing sugar and honey and beat slowly until thoroughly combined.

continued overleaf

Satine's carrot cake
continued

300g (10½oz/scant 2½ cups) plain (all-purpose) flour
2 tsp baking powder
½ tsp bicarbonate of soda (baking soda)
½ tsp ground cinnamon
a pinch of salt
50g (1¾oz) pecans, toasted and finely chopped, to decorate

For the frosting
175g (6¼oz) unsalted butter, softened
400g (14oz/scant 2 cups) cream cheese
175g (6¼oz/1½ cups) icing (powdered) sugar, sifted
4 tbsp runny honey

You will need:
3 x 18cm (7in) round cake tins, greased and bases lined with baking paper

8 Trim the domed tops off the cakes to make them level. Place one cake layer on a serving plate and spread with 3–4 tablespoons of the cream cheese frosting. Cover with a second cake layer. Repeat and then cover the top and sides of the cake with the remaining frosting, spreading it evenly with a palette knife. Chill for 30 minutes.

9 To decorate, push rosemary sprigs or small strips of angelica into the hole at the top of each marzipan carrot. Press the pecans around the base of the cake and around the top edge. Arrange the carrots on the top of the cake to serve.

STORAGE: Can be stored in an airtight box somewhere cool or in the fridge for up to 4 days.

Winston's cheesey scones

Winston the Owl is an aspiring chef who takes his cooking creativity to the next level. His friends inspire his latest culinary delights and he is always ready to whip up his famous mac and cheese.

Makes 16 scones

225ml (7½fl oz/scant 1 cup) whole (full-fat) milk, plus a little extra for brushing
2 tsp lemon juice
350g (12oz/2¾ cups) plain (all-purpose) flour, plus extra for dusting
3 tsp baking powder
125g (4½oz) unsalted butter, chilled and diced
175g (6¼oz) grated mature Cheddar
4 spring onions (scallions), trimmed and finely chopped
1 tbsp finely snipped chives
1 tbsp finely grated Parmesan
salt and freshly ground black pepper

You will need:
baking sheet lined with baking paper

STORAGE: These are best eaten on the day of making and preferably while still slightly warm from the oven.

1 Mix the milk with the lemon juice and set aside for 10 minutes.

2 Sift the flour and baking powder into a large mixing bowl. Season well with freshly ground black pepper and a pinch of salt and add the butter. Rub the butter into the dry ingredients using your fingertips. When there are only very small specks of butter still visible, add all but 2 tablespoons of the Cheddar and mix to combine. Add the spring onions and chives and mix well to combine.

3 Make a well in the middle of the mixture and pour in the milk. Using a palette knife, mix the dough until just combined, then turn out onto a lightly floured work surface and knead very lightly for 10 seconds until combined. Pat the dough into a neat 20 x 30cm (8 x 12in) rectangle with one of the shorter sides nearest to you.

4 Fold the bottom third of the dough up to the middle and the top third down to cover it. Pat or roll the dough out again and repeat this folding.

5 Roll the dough out again into a 20 x 20cm (8 x 8in) square and, using a sharp knife, cut it into 16 squares. Arrange on the lined baking sheet, leaving a little space between each scone to allow for spreading during cooking.

6 Chill the scones for 20 minutes while you preheat the oven to (fan) 190°C/210°C/425°F/gas mark 7.

7 Brush the top of the scones with a little milk, scatter with the remaining Cheddar and the Parmesan and bake on the middle shelf of the oven for 18–20 minutes until well risen and golden brown. Remove from the oven and transfer to a wire rack to cool.

Ash's sprinkle donuts

Ash is a true morning 'Mallow! He can't wait to get up and start creating new beats on his keyboard. A donut helps him start his day and get the music flowing! Sometimes, sprinkles even get stuck on the keys, but Ash doesn't mind. Want to share a donut with Ash?

Makes 12 ring and 12 small round donuts

450g (1lb/3¾ cups) strong white bread flour, plus extra for dusting

75g (2¾oz/⅓ cup) caster (superfine) sugar, plus 250g (9oz/1¼ cups) for coating

7g (¼oz/1¾ tsp) fast-action dried yeast

a pinch of salt

225ml (7½fl oz/scant 1 cup) whole (full-fat) milk, warmed

1 large egg

50g (1¾oz) unsalted butter, softened

1 litre (34fl oz/4 cups) sunflower oil

1 Tip the flour, 75g sugar, yeast and salt into the bowl of a stand mixer fitted with the dough hook. Make a well in the centre of the dry ingredients, add the warm milk, egg and butter and mix on slow speed to combine, then increase the speed to medium and knead for 5–7 minutes until the dough is smooth and elastic. It will still be slightly sticky.

2 Lightly dust a work surface with a little flour, turn the dough out of the bowl and shape it into a smooth ball, then lightly grease the bowl with oil and return the dough to the bowl. Cover with a clean tea towel and leave the dough to prove at room temperature for about 1 hour or until doubled in size.

3 Lightly dust a work surface with flour again and turn the dough out of the bowl. Roll it out to a thickness of just over 1cm (½in). Using the 7cm (2¾in) cutter, stamp out 12 discs from the dough and place on oiled baking trays, leaving plenty of space between each doughnut. Using the 3cm (1¼in) cutter, stamp out a smaller disc from the middle of each doughnut and add them to the trays. Cover loosely with oiled cling film (plastic wrap) and leave to rise at room temperature for 40–45 minutes.

continued overleaf

Ash's sprinkle donuts

continued

For the frosting
500g (1lb 2oz/4½ cups)
  icing (powdered) sugar
1 tbsp freshly squeezed
  lemon juice
pink food colouring paste
edible rainbow sprinkles,
  to serve

You will also need:
stand mixer
7cm (2¾in) round cutter
3cm (1¼in) round cutter
2 baking trays, oiled
tray for caster sugar
large baking sheet
sugar thermometer

4 Heat the oil in a large, shallow saucepan or deep fryer to 170–180°C (340–360°F). Cover a large baking sheet with a triple thickness of kitchen paper and tip the remaining 250g caster sugar into a tray.

5 Carefully drop 3 or 4 donuts at a time into the hot oil and fry for about 2 minutes on each side or until golden brown. Remove from the oil with a slotted spoon and drain thoroughly on the kitchen paper. Make sure that the oil comes back up to temperature before frying the next batch of donuts.

6 Place the cooked donuts in the caster sugar so that the undersides are coated. Remove from the sugar and arrange, sugar side down, on a wire rack then leave to cool to room temperature.

7 To make the frosting, mix the icing sugar with the lemon juice and enough cold water to make a smooth, drizzly frosting. Add a tiny bit of food colouring paste to the frosting and mix until thoroughly combined.

8 Dip the top of each donut in the frosting, scatter with sprinkles and leave for at least 30 minutes before serving.

STORAGE: Best eaten on the day of making.

Clara's granola bars

Have you ever seen a 'Mallow deadlift or power clean? It's time you met Clara! This girl loves to see her friends at the local gym, they call themselves the Sugar Box Gang.

Makes about 20 bars

100g (3½oz/scant ½ cup) coconut oil

75g (2¾oz/⅓ cup) crunchy peanut or almond butter

100g (3½oz/generous ½ cup) soft light brown sugar

100g (3½oz/ scant ½ cup) date or maple syrup

75g (2¾oz) dried apricots, finely chopped

350g (12oz/2¾ cups) rolled oats

75g (2¾oz) sultanas

75g (2¾oz) mixed seeds (pumpkin, sunflower, sesame and linseed)

50g (1¾oz) flaked almonds

25g (1oz) coconut flakes

25g (1oz) cacao nibs

½ tsp ground cinnamon

a pinch of salt

1 ripe banana, peeled and mashed

You will need:

20 x 30cm (8 x 12in) brownie tin, greased and base and sides lined with baking paper

1 Preheat the oven to (fan) 160°C/180°C/350°F/gas mark 4.

2 In a small saucepan, combine the coconut oil, nut butter, brown sugar and date or maple syrup. Place over a low heat and slowly melt the coconut oil and sugar into the syrup, stirring occasionally. Add the apricots to the pan, simmer for 30 seconds, then remove from the heat.

3 In a large bowl combine the oats, sultanas, mixed seeds, flaked almonds, coconut flakes, cacao nibs, ground cinnamon and salt.

4 Add the banana to the bowl with the coconut oil and syrup mixture. Mix well until thoroughly combined, then add to the bowl of dry ingredients and stir to combine. Tip into the prepared brownie tin and press down in a firm and even layer with the back of a spoon. Bake on the middle shelf of the oven for 30–35 minutes until golden.

5 Remove from the oven and leave to cool in the tin for 5 minutes, then cut into 20 squares or bars and leave to cool completely before serving.

STORAGE: Will keep in an airtight box for up to 4 days.

Rosie's shortbread

Meet Rosie, she's visiting her family from the other side of the pond! Rosie loves crunchy biscuits, going to concerts with her friends, and spending time with her nanna. Rosie's nanna makes the best tea and always has yummy treats ready when she comes over.

Makes about 24 shortbreads

150g (5½oz) unsalted butter, softened
75g (2¾oz/⅓ cup) caster (superfine) sugar, plus 1 tbsp extra for dusting
1 tsp vanilla extract or vanilla bean paste
225g (8oz/1¾ cups) plain (all-purpose) flour, plus extra for dusting
1 tsp finely grated lemon zest (from an unwaxed lemon)
a pinch of salt

To decorate
100g (3½oz) milk chocolate, chopped
100g (3½oz) white chocolate, chopped
dried edible flower petals (optional)

You will need:
6cm (2½in) flower or plain round cookie cutter

1 Cream the butter with the sugar and vanilla in a bowl for 2–3 minutes, until pale and light. This is easiest using a stand mixer fitted with the creamer attachment. Scrape down the sides of the bowl with a rubber spatula from time to time.

2 Add the flour, lemon zest and salt and mix to combine, being careful not to overwork the dough. Shape the mixture into a ball, flatten into a disc, wrap in cling film (plastic wrap) and chill for 1 hour until firm.

3 Very lightly dust a work surface with flour, unwrap the dough and roll it out to a thickness of about 5mm (¼in). Use a 6cm (2½in) cutter to stamp out about 24 shapes and arrange on baking paper-lined baking sheets. Sprinkle with the extra sugar and chill for 20 minutes.

4 Meanwhile, preheat the oven to (fan) 130°C/150°C/300°F/gas mark 2.

5 Bake the shortbread on the middle shelf of the oven for about 25 minutes until firm and just starting to turn light golden at the edges. Leave to cool on the baking sheet for 10 minutes, then carefully slide onto a wire rack to cool completely.

6 Tip the chopped chocolate into two separate medium heatproof bowls and melt either over a pan of barely simmering water (being careful to ensure the bottom of the bowl isn't touching the water) or in the microwave on a low setting, stirring from time to time. Half dip the shortbreads into either the milk or white chocolate, then scatter with edible dried flowers (if using) and leave to set before serving.

STORAGE: Will keep in an airtight box for up to 4 days.

SUMMER
VIBES

Belton's mini lemon drizzle cakes

Meet Belton. They work at the local bookstore and have a passion for old books and mythical stories. Sometimes when Belton is at the bookstore at night, they say they can hear the books talk! Do you want to dive into the historical, mythical world of the bookstore with Belton?

Makes 12 mini cakes

175g (6¼oz) unsalted
   butter, softened
175g (6¼oz/generous ¾ cup)
   caster (superfine) sugar
3 medium eggs,
   lightly beaten
finely grated zest and juice
   from 2 unwaxed lemons
175g (6¼oz/1½ cups) plain
   (all-purpose) flour
2 tsp baking powder
a pinch of salt
50g (1¾oz/scant ½ cup)
   ground almonds
   (almond meal)
2 tbsp whole (full-fat) milk
5 tbsp granulated sugar

1 Preheat the oven to (fan) 160°C/180°C/350°F/gas mark 4.

2 Cream the butter and sugar together until pale and light. This is easiest using a stand mixer fitted with the creamer attachment and will take 3–4 minutes on medium speed.

3 Gradually add the eggs, mixing well between each addition and scraping down the sides of the bowl from time to time with a rubber spatula. Add the lemon zest to the cake mixture.

4 Sift the flour, baking powder and salt into the bowl, add the ground almonds and fold into the cake mixture using a large metal spoon or rubber spatula until the mixture is smooth. Add the juice from 1 of the lemons and the milk and mix again to combine.

5 Divide the cake batter evenly among the mini sandwich tins and spread level with a teaspoon. Bake on the middle shelf of the oven for about 20 minutes until golden, well risen and a skewer inserted into the middle of the cakes comes out clean.

6 Remove from the oven. Mix the juice from the remaining lemon with the granulated sugar and brush over the tops of the hot cakes.

continued overleaf

Belton's mini lemon drizzle cakes

continued

For the filling

1 quantity of regular
   buttercream
   (see page 128)
finely grated zest and juice
   of ½ unwaxed lemon
3 tbsp lemon curd
icing (powdered) sugar,
   for dusting

You will need:

stand mixer
12-hole mini Victoria sponge
   tin or muffin tin, greased
piping (pastry) bag fitted
   with a medium star nozzle

7 Leave the cakes to rest in the tin for 5 minutes, then carefully ease them out onto a wire rack and leave until cold.

8 To make the buttercream filling, follow the instructions on page 128, adding the lemon zest and juice at the end, then mixing again to combine. Scoop the buttercream into the piping bag.

9 Cut the cakes in half horizontally and spread the bottom layer with lemon curd, then pipe the buttercream on top. Sandwich with the top cake layers and lightly dust with icing sugar to serve.

TIP: If you don't have a mini cake tin then simply use a muffin tin, greased with butter and dusted with a little flour. Or make one large cake using a deep 20cm (8in) round cake tin and bake for about 40 minutes.

STORAGE: Store in an airtight box for up to 4 days.

Tenise's pineapple upside down cake

Meet Tenise. He just moved to the big city from the jungle! Change can be scary, but he's already met so many new 'Mallows! Tenise works at a bakery and makes the best pineapple coconut cakes in town. Want to give it a try?

Makes 1 large cake (serves 8–10)

2 x 425g (15oz) tins pineapple rings in juice

75g (2¾oz/⅓ cup) soft light brown sugar

300g (10½oz) unsalted butter, softened, plus extra for greasing

12 glacé cherries

255g (9oz/1¼ cups) caster (superfine) sugar

4 medium eggs, lightly beaten

1 tsp vanilla extract or vanilla bean paste

250g (9oz/2 cups) plain (all-purpose) flour

2½ tsp baking powder

a pinch of salt

2 tbsp whole (full-fat) milk

You will need:

solid-bottomed 23cm (9in) cake tin, base and sides greased and base lined with baking paper

1 Preheat the oven to (fan) 160°C/180°C/350°F/gas mark 4, then drain the pineapple rings and leave to dry on kitchen paper while you prepare the cake.

2 Combine the soft light brown sugar and 75g (2¾oz) of the unsalted butter in a small saucepan and melt over a medium heat. Spoon into the bottom of the prepared cake tin. Cut the pineapple rings in half to make semi-circles and arrange them around the edges of the tin – you may only need 8 of the pineapple rings for this, depending on how tightly you pack the slices in. Place the remaining slices in the middle of the tin. Arrange glacé cherries in between each pineapple slice.

3 Using a stand mixer, cream the remaining 225g (8oz) butter and the caster sugar until pale and light, scraping down the sides of the bowl from time to time. Gradually add the beaten eggs, mixing well between each addition, then add the vanilla and mix again. Sift the flour, baking powder and salt into the bowl, add the milk and mix again until the cake mixture is smooth and thoroughly combined.

4 Carefully spoon the mixture into the prepared tin on top of the pineapple slices and cherries, spread level and bake on the middle shelf of the oven for 45–50 minutes until well risen, golden brown and a skewer inserted into the middle of the cake comes out clean.

5 Remove from the oven and leave to rest in the tin for 2 minutes, then carefully turn the cake out onto a serving plate and leave to cool.

STORAGE: Will keep in an airtight box for up to 2 days.

Jyri's peach and almond traybake

Jyri has a serious sweet tooth. He treats himself to cake, tartlets, and cookies all the time. Jyri knows his limit, but sometimes he just can't help himself and he eats too many pastries – the sugar rush really pushes back his bedtime!

Serves 8

For the streusel topping
35g (1¼oz) unsalted butter, chilled and diced
35g (1¼oz/scant ¼ cup) soft light brown sugar
35g (1¼oz/generous ¼ cup) plain (all-purpose) flour
35g (1¼oz/¼ cup) ground almonds (almond meal)
a pinch of salt
35g (1¼oz) flaked almonds

For the cake
200g (7oz) unsalted butter, softened
200g (7oz/1 cup) caster (superfine) sugar

1 Preheat the oven to (fan) 160°C/180°C/350°F/gas mark 4.

2 Start by making the streusel topping. Tip the 35g butter, soft light brown sugar, flour, ground almonds and salt into a mixing bowl. Rub the butter into the dry ingredients with your fingertips until the mixture starts to clump together. Add the flaked almonds, mix to combine and then set aside while you prepare the cake mixture.

3 Combine the 200g butter and caster sugar in a stand mixer fitted with the creamer attachment and beat until light and fluffy. Gradually add the beaten eggs, mixing well after each addition and scraping down the sides of the bowl. Add the vanilla and lemon zest and mix to combine. Sift the flour, baking powder, bicarbonate of soda and salt into the mixture, add the ground almonds and soured cream and mix again to thoroughly combine.

4 Spoon the mixture into the prepared tin and smooth the top. Quarter the peaches and cut into 3mm (⅛in)-thick slices. Arrange two-thirds of the sliced peaches on top of the cake mixture and scatter with the

continued overleaf

Jyri's peach and almond traybake

continued

3 medium eggs, lightly beaten
2 tsp vanilla extract or vanilla bean paste
finely grated zest of ½ unwaxed lemon
150g (5½oz/1¼ cups) plain (all-purpose) flour
1½ tsp baking powder
½ tsp bicarbonate of soda (baking soda)
a pinch of salt
100g (3½oz/scant 1 cup) ground almonds (almond meal)
150g (5½oz/scant ¾ cup) soured cream
3 large ripe peaches
icing (powdered) sugar, for dusting

To serve
ice cream or crème fraîche

You will need:
stand mixer
20 x 30cm (8 x 12in) brownie tin, base and sides greased and lined with baking paper

streusel topping. Nestle the remaining peaches around then bake on the middle shelf of the oven for about 40 minutes, or until a skewer inserted into the middle of the cake comes out with a moist crumb.

5 Remove from the oven and allow the cake to cool in the tin. Dust with icing sugar and serve with ice cream or crème fraîche.

STORAGE: Best eaten on the day of making.

Cam's three-colour dough cookies

Cam loves to jump in and out of boxes, and build forts with his friends Hoot and Wendy. He also loves going to the beach to take cat naps with his friends but is always up for an adventure!

Makes about 20 cookies

For the vanilla dough

200g (7oz) unsalted butter, softened

125g (4½oz/scant 1¼ cups) icing (powdered) sugar

2 medium eggs, lightly beaten

75g (2¾oz/¾ cup) ground almonds (almond meal)

¼ tsp baking powder

a pinch of salt

1 tsp vanilla extract or vanilla bean paste

150g (5½oz/1¼ cups) plain (all-purpose) flour, sifted

For the dark chocolate dough

65g (2oz/generous ½ cup) plain (all-purpose) flour, sifted

15g (½oz/3 tsp) cocoa powder, sifted

1 Start making the vanilla dough. Using a stand mixer fitted with the creamer attachment, beat together the butter and sugar for 2–3 minutes until pale and light.

2 Gradually add the beaten eggs, scraping down the sides of the bowl with a spatula, and mix again until combined. Add the ground almonds, baking powder and salt and mix to combine using a rubber spatula.

3 Weigh the mixture and scoop half of the total weight into a bowl. Add the vanilla and 150g (5½oz/1¼ cups) flour to this and mix with the rubber spatula until smooth and thoroughly combined. Shape the vanilla dough into a log, wrap in cling film (plastic wrap) and chill.

4 Divide the remaining mixture into two equal portions. One portion will be the dark chocolate dough – so add 65g (2oz/generous ½ cup) flour and 15g (½oz/3 tsp) cocoa powder and mix with the rubber spatula to combine. Shape into a log, wrap in cling film and chill.

5 For the light chocolate dough, add the 75g (2¾oz/⅔ cup) flour and 5g (⅛oz/1 tsp) cocoa powder to the final portion of mixture, mix to combine, shape into a log and cover. Chill all of the dough mixtures for about 1 hour or until firm.

continued overleaf

Cam's three-colour dough cookies
continued

For the light chocolate dough
75g (2¾oz/⅔ cup) plain (all-purpose) flour, sifted
5g (⅛oz/1 tsp) cocoa powder, sifted

You will need:
stand mixer
2 baking sheets lined with baking paper
5cm (2in) round cookie cutter

6 Unwrap each log of chilled dough and, using your hands, roll each log into ropes 2–3cm (¾–1¼in) wide – they should all be of equal thickness, and you will have twice as much vanilla dough as the others. Cut each rope into 3cm (1¼in) lengths and arrange the pieces on the lined baking sheet so that the colours form a random pattern and are all pressing up against each other. Cover with another sheet of baking paper and gently roll out to a thickness of 3mm (⅛in). The colours should all squash together to form a three-colour dough. Chill for 20 minutes.

7 Using the cookie cutter, stamp out as many discs as you can from the dough – you should get about 20 – and arrange on the lined baking sheet, leaving a little space between each one. Gather the dough scraps together, re-roll and stamp out more discs – by now the three colours will be more marbled.

8 Chill for 20 minutes while preheating the oven to (fan) 150°C/170°C/ 325°F/gas mark 3.

9 Bake the cookies for 10–12 minutes until they are firm and only just starting to brown at the edges. Remove from the oven and leave to cool on the baking sheet.

STORAGE: Will keep for up to 1 week in an airtight box.

Melina's peanut butter cookies

Baking is one of Melina's favorite things to do, her second is eating the sweet treats she bakes. She takes advantage of all eight tentacles in the kitchen and makes some of the best peanut butter cookies you'll ever try.

Makes about 24 cookies

125g (4½oz) unsalted butter, softened

100g (3½oz/generous ½ cup) soft light brown sugar

75g (2¾oz/⅓ cup) golden caster (superfine) sugar, plus 75g (2¾oz/⅓ cup) for rolling cookies

1 medium egg, lightly beaten

1 tsp vanilla extract or vanilla bean paste

175g (6¼oz/¾ cups) crunchy peanut butter

175g (6¼oz/1½ cups) plain (all-purpose) flour

½ tsp bicarbonate of soda (baking soda)

a pinch of salt

50g (1¾oz) salted peanuts, roughly chopped

You will need:

stand mixer

2 baking sheets lined with baking paper

1 Cream the butter with the light brown sugar and 75g (2¾oz/⅓ cup) golden caster sugar in a stand mixer fitted with the creamer attachment for about 3 minutes until pale and light. Scrape down the sides of the mixer bowl with a rubber spatula, add the egg and vanilla and mix for 1 minute to thoroughly combine.

2 Add the peanut butter and mix until smooth. Sift the flour, bicarbonate of soda and salt into the bowl and mix for a further 30 seconds until smooth and combined. Scoop the dough into a clean bowl, then cover and chill for 2 hours until firm.

3 Preheat the oven to (fan) 150°C/170°C/325°F/gas mark 3.

4 Tip the remaining caster sugar onto a plate. Roll tablespoons of chilled cookie dough into neat balls in your hands, roll the dough balls in the caster sugar to coat and place on the lined baking sheets, leaving space between each cookie to allow for spreading during cooking (the mixture should make about 24 cookies). Using your fingers slightly flatten the dough balls and press the tines of a fork in a criss-cross pattern in the top of each cookie. Scatter the tops of the cookies with the peanuts.

5 Bake in the oven on the middle shelf for about 12 minutes until golden brown. Leave to cool for 2 minutes on the baking sheets then transfer to a wire rack and leave until cold before serving.

STORAGE: Will keep in an airtight box for up to 4 days.

Deacon's jewelled ice cream cake

Sunday night ice cream sundae parties are at Deacon's house! Any time is a good time for ice cream, and Deacon loves to start off his week with triple scoops of rocky road, rainbow sprinkles, and extra cherries. Want to join Deacon's Sunday sundae party?

Makes 1 cake (serves 8–10)

4 medium eggs
100g (3½oz/½ cup) caster (superfine) sugar
1 tsp vanilla extract or vanilla bean paste
100g (3½oz/¾ cup) plain (all-purpose) flour
½ tsp baking powder
a pinch of salt
30g (1¼oz) unsalted butter, melted

For the chocolate fudge sauce

125ml (4fl oz/½ cup) double (heavy) cream
75g (2¾oz/⅓ cup) soft light brown sugar
100g (3½oz) 70% dark (bittersweet) chocolate, chopped
25g (1oz) unsalted butter
1 tsp vanilla extract or vanilla bean paste
a pinch of salt

1 Preheat the oven to (fan) 160°C/180°C/350°F/gas mark 4.

2 To make the sponge layers, whisk the eggs, sugar and vanilla in a stand mixer fitted with the whisk attachment for 3–4 minutes until pale, doubled in volume and the mixture holds a firm ribbon trail when the whisk is lifted from the bowl. Sift the flour, baking powder and salt into the bowl and fold them in using a large metal spoon or rubber spatula. Pour the melted butter around the edge of the mixture and fold in.

3 Divide the mixture evenly between the three lined cake tins, gently spread level and bake for about 14 minutes until golden and the cakes spring back when pressed lightly with a fingertip. Remove from the oven and leave to cool for 2–3 minutes, then remove from the tins and leave on a wire rack until cold.

4 Meanwhile, make the chocolate fudge sauce. Combine all the ingredients in a small saucepan over a low heat, stirring constantly until smooth. Remove from the heat and leave to cool at room temperature until ready to assemble the cake.

5 Line the inside of the deep cake tin with the acetate strip. Place one cake layer in the bottom of the tin and spread the top of the cake with 1 tablespoon of chocolate fudge sauce, leaving a 1cm (½in) border around the edge. Pop in the freezer for 20 minutes.

continued overleaf

Deacon's jewelled ice cream cake *continued*

For the filling and topping
1 x 500g (1lb 2oz) tub
   strawberry ice cream
1 x 500g (1lb 2oz) tub
   pistachio or mint ice cream
400ml (13½fl oz/1⅔ cups)
   double (heavy) cream
edible sprinkles
seeds from ½ pomegranate
handful of fresh redcurrants

You will need:
stand mixer
3 x 15cm (6in) round cake
   tins, greased and bases
   lined with baking paper
deep 15cm (6in) round cake tin
50 x 12cm (20 x 4¾in) strip
   of acetate
hand-held electric whisk

6 Meanwhile, remove the strawberry ice cream from the freezer and leave for 10 minutes to soften slightly. Spoon the ice cream into the cake tin on top of the first cake layer and spread it level with the back of the spoon. Press the second cake layer on top, spread with fudge sauce and return to the freezer for 30 minutes. Slightly soften the pistachio (or mint) ice cream and spoon on top of the second cake layer. Top with the third and final cake layer and press together. Freeze for at least 1 hour until solid.

7 Whip the cream with a hand-held electric whisk until it holds firm peaks. Remove the cake from the tin, peel off the acetate and place on a serving plate. Using a palette knife, cover the top and sides of the cake with whipped cream and return to the freezer for 30 minutes.

8 Scatter with edible sprinkles, pomegranate seeds and redcurrants and serve with any remaining fudge sauce, slightly warmed, for pouring.

STORAGE: Will keep for up to 1 week in the freezer.

Cruz's avocado cupcakes

Mini golf and guacamole are two things that Cruz the sun can't live without, he'd play mini golf every day if he could! He likes guac on everything from breakfast and sandwiches to his mom's healthy avocado cupcakes!

Makes 12 cupcakes

150ml (5fl oz/⅔ cup) whole (full-fat) milk
juice of ½ lemon
1 ripe avocado (115–125g/ 4–4½oz peeled flesh)
175g (6¼oz/generous ¾ cup) caster (superfine) sugar
2 medium eggs, lightly beaten
1 tsp vanilla extract or vanilla bean paste
green food colouring paste (optional)
200g (7oz/1⅔ cups) plain (all-purpose) flour
1 tsp baking powder
1 tsp bicarbonate of soda (baking soda)
a pinch of salt

For the frosting
2 ripe avocados (250g/9oz peeled flesh)
3 tbsp cocoa powder, sifted
4 tbsp icing (powdered) sugar, sifted
4 tbsp agave or maple syrup

To decorate
25g (1oz) pistachios, finely chopped
a handful of blueberries
1 kiwi fruit, peeled

You will need:
12-hole muffin tin lined with paper cases
small blender
piping (pastry) bag fitted with a medium star nozzle

1 Preheat the oven to (fan) 160°C/180°C/350°F/gas mark 4.

2 Pour the milk into a jug, add the lemon juice, whisk to combine and set aside for 10 minutes.

3 Cut the avocado in half, remove the stone and scrape the flesh into a mixing bowl. Using a fork, mash the avocado until smooth. Add the caster sugar and mix with a balloon whisk for about 1 minute until thoroughly combined. Gradually add the beaten eggs, mixing well between each addition. Add the vanilla and a tiny drop of green food colouring paste (if using) and mix to combine.

4 Sift the flour, baking powder, bicarbonate of soda and salt into the bowl and whisk until almost incorporated. Add the milk and lemon mixture, then beat again until the cake mixture is smooth.

5 Divide the mixture evenly between the paper cases and bake in the oven for about 20 minutes, until well risen and a skewer inserted into the middle of the cakes comes out clean. Remove from the oven and leave the cupcakes to cool in the tin for 5 minutes, then transfer to a wire rack until cold.

6 To make the frosting, purée the avocado flesh in a small blender until smooth. Add the cocoa powder, sugar and agave or maple syrup and blend again until silky smooth. Scoop the mixture into the piping bag and pipe over the top of each cupcake. Scatter with chopped pistachios and thinly sliced blueberries and kiwi fruit to serve.

STORAGE: Best eaten on the day of making.

Genevieve's macarons

Have you seen Genevieve roll by? She's the cat in the glitter roller skates! If you can't find her skating around with her squad, you might want to check the bakery. Genevieve absolutely loves macarons and how pretty they look on display!

Makes about 30 macarons

For the macaron shells

175g (6¼oz/1½ cups) ground almonds (almond meal)

175g (6¼oz/1½ cups) icing (powdered) sugar

130–150g (4½–5½oz) egg whites (save 2 yolks for the filling)

a pinch of salt

175g (6¼oz/generous ¾ cup) caster (superfine) sugar

½ tsp green food colouring paste

For the chocolate filling

100g (3½oz) dark (bittersweet) chocolate, chopped

50g (1¾oz/¼ cup) caster (superfine) sugar

2 egg yolks

125g (4½oz) unsalted butter, softened

1 Twist one of the piping bags just above the nozzle and sit the bag in a large jug so that the top is folded back and open wide.

2 Tip the ground almonds and icing sugar into a food processor and blitz for 30 seconds to 1 minute to thoroughly mix. Sift the mixture into a large mixing bowl and set aside.

3 Tip half of the egg whites and the salt into a large heatproof mixing bowl (or bowl of a stand mixer) and set aside.

4 Combine the caster sugar with 2 tablespoons of water and set the pan over a low–medium heat to dissolve the sugar. Bring to the boil and cook the syrup for about 2 minutes until it reaches 118°C (244°F) on a sugar thermometer. Meanwhile, start whisking the egg whites in the mixer bowl until they are stiff and white but not dry.

5 Slide the pan off the heat and slowly and carefully pour the hot syrup into the egg whites, whisking continuously on slow speed. Increase the speed of the mixer and continue mixing for about 2 minutes until the meringue is cooled, glossy and stiff.

6 Add the remaining egg whites to the almond and icing sugar mixture and beat until smooth. Add the food colouring paste and mix until thoroughly combined.

7 Using a rubber spatula, fold one third of the meringue into the almond mixture until smooth. Add another third of the meringue and fold in. Repeat with the remaining meringue and continue folding until the mixture resembles thick molten lava that will hold a ribbon trail for about 5 seconds.

continued overleaf

Genevieve's macarons continued

continued

You will need:
food processor
sugar thermometer
2 large baking sheets lined
   with silicon baking mats
   or baking paper
2 large piping (pastry) bags
   fitted with 1cm (½in)
   plain nozzles

8 Scoop the mixture into the prepared piping bag and pipe 30 even-sized macarons onto each lined baking sheet. Sharply bang the baking sheets on the work surface to pop any air bubbles and set aside for about 30 minutes until a light skin has formed on the surface of each macaron shell.

9 Preheat the oven to (fan) 150°C/170°C/325°F/gas mark 3.

10 Bake the macarons on the middle shelf of the oven for about 15 minutes until well risen and crisp with well-defined 'feet'. Remove from the oven and leave to cool completely on the baking sheets while you prepare the chocolate filling.

11 Melt the chocolate in a heatproof bowl over a pan of barely simmering water (being careful to ensure the bottom of the bowl isn't touching the water), stir until smooth and remove from the heat. Combine the caster sugar, egg yolks and 1 tablespoon of water in another heatproof bowl, place over the pan of barely simmering water and whisk continuously for about 3 minutes until the egg yolks are pale and thickened slightly. Remove the bowl from the heat and continue to whisk until the mixture is cool. Add the butter a little at a time, beating constantly. Add the melted chocolate and beat until smooth and thoroughly combined. Spoon into a second piping bag and leave at room temperature to cool and thicken before piping.

12 To assemble the macarons, turn half of the shells over so that they are flat side uppermost and pipe with a teaspoon of chocolate filling. Top with another shell, pressing them gently together so that the cream is visible from the sides. Place the macarons on a tray, cover with cling film (plastic wrap) and chill overnight before serving.

STORAGE: Will keep in an airtight box in the fridge for up to 4 days.

Sassafras's chocolate orange Bundt cakes

Sassafras bakes all kinds of doughy delights, but confetti cakes are her speciality. There's nothing like a dessert from the kitchen of Sassafras, because she never writes down a recipe! This 'Mallow uses her keen sense of smell to know exactly when a baked treat is ready to pull from the oven.

Makes 6 individual cakes

For the cakes

20g (¾oz) unsalted butter, melted, plus extra for greasing

100ml (3½fl oz/scant ½ cup) sunflower oil

finely grated zest and juice of 1 orange

2 medium eggs

75g (2¾oz/⅓ cup) soured cream

100g (3½oz/½ cup) golden caster (superfine) sugar

100g (3½oz/½ cup) soft light brown sugar

100g (3½oz) dark (bittersweet) chocolate, chopped and melted

1 Thoroughly brush the inside of the Bundt tins with melted butter to cover every surface. Dust the tins with plain flour, tapping out the excess.

2 Preheat the oven to (fan) 160°C/180°C/350°F/gas mark 4.

3 In a mixing bowl combine the butter, sunflower oil, orange zest and juice, eggs, soured cream and both sugars and beat using a balloon whisk until smooth and thoroughly combined. Add the melted chocolate and mix again. Sift the flour, cocoa, baking powder, bicarbonate of soda and salt into the bowl and whisk until thoroughly combined. Add the boiling water and mix again until smooth.

4 Scoop into a jug and pour the mixture evenly among the prepared tins. Bake in the oven on the middle shelf for about 25 minutes until well risen and a skewer inserted into the middle of the cakes comes out clean.

5 Remove from the oven and leave the cakes to cool in the tins for 4–5 minutes, then carefully remove from the tins and leave to cool completely on a wire rack.

continued overleaf

Sassafras's chocolate orange Bundt cakes
continued

150g (5½oz/1¼ cups) plain (all-purpose) flour, plus extra for dusting

25g (1oz/3½ tbsp) cocoa powder

½ tsp baking powder

½ tsp bicarbonate of soda (baking soda)

a pinch of salt

50ml (1¾fl oz/3½ tbsp) boiling water

For the frosting

75g (2¾oz/⅓ cup) soft light brown sugar

50g (1¾oz/scant ¼ cup) dark muscovado sugar

50g (1¾oz) unsalted butter

1 tsp finely grated orange zest

100ml (3½fl oz/scant ½ cup) double (heavy) cream

100g (3½oz) dark (bittersweet) chocolate, chopped

a large pinch of salt

For the candied orange peel

1 large orange, unwaxed, washed

75g (2¾oz/⅓ cup) caster (superfine) sugar

You will need:

6 individual Bundt tins

balloon whisk

6 To make the frosting, combine the sugars, butter, orange zest and cream in a small saucepan. Heat gently to dissolve the sugar and melt the butter and bring to the boil. Simmer for 30 seconds, remove from the heat and add the chocolate and salt. Stir until the chocolate has melted and the sauce is silky smooth.

7 Carefully spoon the sauce over the cold cakes, allowing it to drizzle over the sides, and leave to set before serving.

8 To make the candied orange peel, remove the peel from the orange using a vegetable peeler and cut it into fine strips. Tip the sugar onto a baking tray or large plate, add the orange zest strips and mix to coat. Leave uncovered at room temperature for about 3 hours or until crisp, turning the zest in the sugar from time to time.

9 Remove the candied orange peel from the sugar and arrange over the top of the cakes to serve.

STORAGE: Will keep in an airtight box for up to 3 days.

Rei's chocolate avocado tart

Have you ever met a Pegasus who loves avocados? Well, now you have! Rei is the life of the party and spends her free time at the beach. She loves blowing bubbles at sunset and then dancing and singing with her friends in the moonlight.

Serves 8

For the base
300g (10½oz) chocolate cream sandwich biscuits (Oreos)
75g (2¾oz) unsalted butter

For the filling
200g (7oz) 70% dark (bittersweet) chocolate, chopped
3 medium-sized ripe avocados
200ml (7fl oz/generous ¾ cup) coconut cream
1 tbsp cocoa or cacao powder
100ml (3½fl oz/scant ½ cup) maple syrup
1 tbsp smooth almond butter

To decorate
3 ripe figs, sliced
100g (3½oz) blueberries
150g (5½oz) blackberries

You will need:
food processor or blender
20cm (8in) tart or flan ring or fluted tart tin with a removable base
baking sheet lined with baking paper

1 Preheat the oven to (fan) 170°C/190°C/375°F/gas mark 5.

2 Crush the chocolate biscuits to a crumb either in a freezer bag, using a rolling pin to bash them, or in a food processor, then tip them into a mixing bowl. Melt the butter, add to the biscuit crumbs and mix well to thoroughly combine.

3 If using a tart ring without a base, place it on a lined baking sheet. Firmly press the crumb mixture into the tart ring or fluted tart tin to evenly cover the base and sides. Bake on the middle shelf of the oven for 7–8 minutes until crisp. If the crumb crust slumps down the sides of the tin slightly during baking simply press it back into position using the back of a teaspoon. Remove from the oven and leave to cool.

4 To make the filling, melt the chocolate in a heatproof bowl either over a pan of barely simmering water (being careful to ensure the bottom of the bowl isn't touching the water) or in the microwave on a low setting. Stir until smooth, remove from the heat and leave to cool while you prepare the remaining ingredients.

5 Cut the avocados in half, remove the stones and scoop the flesh into a food processor or blender. Add the coconut cream, cocoa powder, maple syrup and almond butter and blend until smooth. Scoop the mixture into the bowl of melted chocolate and mix to thoroughly combine. Spoon into the biscuit crust and spread level using a spoon or palette knife.

6 Chill for 30 minutes to 1 hour or until set, then carefully remove the tart ring, place the tart on a serving plate and decorate with figs, blueberries and blackberries.

STORAGE: Best on the day of making, but can be covered and stored in the fridge for up to 2 days.

Rutabaga's chocolate chip cookie cups

Have you ever met a caterpillar who can't live without chocolate? Peanut butter cups and chocolate chip cookies are two of Rutabaga's favorite treats. And if you're making cookies, Rutabaga has just one rule to follow: always add more chocolate chips.

Makes 12 cookie cups

100g (3½oz) unsalted butter, at room temperature
50g (1¾oz) peanut butter
75g (2¾oz/⅓ cup) soft light brown sugar
75g (2¾oz/generous ⅓ cup) caster (superfine) sugar
1 medium egg, lightly beaten
1 tsp vanilla extract or vanilla bean paste
175g (6¼oz/1½ cups) plain (all-purpose) flour
1 tsp bicarbonate of soda (baking soda)
150g (5½oz) chocolate chips (dark or milk, or a combination)
50g (1¾oz) salted peanuts, roughly chopped, plus extra to decorate
12 mini peanut butter cups or 12 tsp chocolate hazelnut spread

You will need:
stand mixer or hand-held electric whisk
12-hole muffin tin, greased and each base lined with a disc of baking paper

STORAGE: Can be stored in an airtight box for up to 4 days.

1 Preheat the oven to (fan) 160°C/180°C/350°F/gas mark 4.

2 Using a stand mixer or hand-held electric whisk, cream the butter and peanut butter in a bowl with both the sugars until pale and light. Add the beaten egg and vanilla and mix well to combine. Sift the flour and bicarbonate of soda into the bowl and mix until almost combined. Add the chocolate chips and chopped peanuts and mix again until evenly distributed throughout the dough.

3 Weigh the dough and divide evenly among the muffin tin holes. Flatten the top of each cookie cup and bake on the middle shelf of the oven for about 15 minutes until the cookies are golden brown but the middle is still very slightly soft. They will crisp up further on cooling.

4 Place one peanut butter cup on top of each hot cookie cup, leave to melt slightly for 5 minutes and then use a palette knife to transfer the cookie cups to a wire rack, scatter with chopped peanuts and leave until cool. If you don't have peanut butter cups, top each cold cookie cup with a teaspoon of chocolate hazelnut spread.

Elizabeth's unicorn cake

Elizabeth is an amazing pastry artist. She is the go-to baker for all the 'Mallow birthday cakes! When she's not wowing us with her baking skills, you can find her travelling with her family.

Makes 1 large cake (serves 12)

For the cake
275g (9¾oz) unsalted butter, softened
275g (9¾oz/scant 1½ cups) caster (superfine) sugar
2 tsp vanilla extract or vanilla bean paste
4 medium eggs
275g (9¾oz/generous 2 cups) plain (all-purpose) flour
3 tsp baking powder
a pinch of salt
3 tbsp whole (full-fat) milk
pink food colouring paste

For the horn and ears
50g (1¾oz) white chocolate, chopped
1 wafer ice cream cone
edible sprinkles, plus extra to decorate
75g (2¾oz) white fondant icing
pink food colouring paste

1 Preheat the oven to (fan) 160°C/180°C/350°F/gas mark 4.

2 To make the cake, combine the butter with the sugar in a stand mixer fitted with the creamer attachment and beat for 3–4 minutes until pale and light. Scrape down the sides of the mixer bowl with a rubber spatula, add the vanilla and mix again to combine. Add the eggs one at a time, mixing well between each addition. Scrape down the sides of the mixer bowl again.

3 Sift the flour, baking powder and salt into the bowl, add the milk and mix on low speed to combine until silky smooth. Weigh the mixture and divide it between two bowls. Tint one half pink using a little food colouring paste, mix until thoroughly combined and spoon into one of the cake tins. Spoon the plain cake mix into the other tin. Spread both mixtures level and bake in the oven for about 30 minutes until well risen, golden and a skewer inserted into the middle of the cakes comes out clean.

4 Remove from the oven and leave to cool in the tins for 10 minutes, then carefully turn out onto a wire rack and leave until cold.

5 To make the unicorn horn, melt the white chocolate in a heatproof bowl either over a pan of barely simmering water (making sure the bowl doesn't touch the water) or in the microwave on a low setting. Stir until smooth. Using a pastry brush, spread the melted chocolate over the outside of the ice cream cone in an even layer. Scatter with edible sprinkles, place upright on a plate and chill until the chocolate has set.

continued overleaf

Elizabeth's unicorn cake
continued

continued

For the meringue buttercream
1.5 quantity of meringue
 buttercream
 (see page 128)
assorted food colouring
 pastes, including pink

You will need:
stand mixer
2 x 15cm (6in) deep cake
 tins, base and sides
 greased and bases lined
 with baking paper
50 x 15cm (20 x 6in) strip
 of acetate
cake decorating turntable
cake side scraper
6 medium disposable
 piping (pastry) bags
2 medium star nozzles
2 small star nozzles

6 To make the ears, divide the fondant icing in half and press and shape each piece into a unicorn ear shape. Brush the inside of the ear with pink food colouring and leave at room temperature for at least 1 hour to firm up.

7 Make the meringue buttercream following the recipe on page 128.

8 To assemble the cake, line the inside of one of the cake tins with the acetate strip. Using a serrated knife, cut the domed top off each cake and then cut the cakes in half horizontally to make 4 layers of even thickness. Place one white cake layer in the bottom of the tin and spread the top with 2–3 tablespoons of the meringue buttercream. Place a pink cake layer on top and spread with a little of the buttercream (you will need to leave enough to cover the sides and top). Continue layering up the cake with buttercream, ending with a pink cake layer. Press the cakes together and chill for 30 minutes.

9 Remove the cake from the tin and peel off the acetate. Place the cake either on a flat plate or a cake board and place on the cake decorating turntable. Cover the top and sides of the cake with a thin layer of buttercream (a crumb coat) and spread smooth using either a cake side scraper or off-set palette knife. Chill again for about 30 minutes until firm.

10 Spoon 4 tablespoons of buttercream into a bowl and tint pink using food colouring paste, then spoon into a disposable piping bag. Spoon about one third of the remaining buttercream into another piping bag. Snip the end of each piping bag to make a 1cm (½in)-wide hole.

11 Place the cake back on the turntable and pipe pink buttercream in concentric rings to come about a quarter of the way up the side of the cake from the bottom. Pipe white buttercream in concentric rings from the top of the pink buttercream and up the sides to the top of the cake. Spread the buttercream smoothly over the sides of the cake using either the scraper or a palette knife, lightly marbling the pink and white icing together. Cover the top of the cake in a smooth layer of white buttercream. Press edible sprinkles around the bottom edge of the cake and chill again for 20 minutes.

12 Divide the remaining buttercream between 3 or 4 bowls and tint each bowl a different colour – pinks, lilac and peachy tones work well. Spoon each coloured buttercream into a separate piping bag fitted with a star nozzle and twist the ends to seal. Pipe rosettes of coloured buttercream to make the unicorn mane and forelock.

13 Position the unicorn horn and ears on top of the cake to serve.

STORAGE: Can be stored in an airtight box in the fridge for up to 2 days.

Robb's banana loaf

Ready to meet Robb? This orangutan's love for cleaning means his house is always picture-perfect. When he's not vacuuming or keeping the house tidy for his family, he's getting wild with his friends. In fact, he's known as 'Local Robb' around town because he's never met a stranger!

Makes 1 large cake (serves 8)

125g (4½oz) unsalted butter, melted
1 tbsp demerara sugar
75g (2¾oz/⅓ cup) soft light brown sugar
50g (1¾oz/¼ cup) caster (superfine) sugar
2 large eggs
100g (3½oz/scant ½ cup) natural yoghurt
2 tsp vanilla extract or vanilla bean paste
3 very ripe medium bananas (peeled weight 200–225g/7–8oz)
250g (9oz/2 cups) self-raising flour
1 tsp baking powder
½ tsp ground cinnamon
a pinch of salt
100g (3½oz) dark (bittersweet) chocolate chips

To decorate
1 banana
1 tbsp demerara sugar

You will need:
1 x 900g (2lb) loaf tin

STORAGE: Can be stored in an airtight box for up to 3 days.

1 Preheat the oven to (fan) 160°C/180°C/350°F/gas mark 4.

2 Brush the loaf tin with a little of the melted butter and line the base and ends with a strip of baking paper. Brush with butter again and dust the base and sides with the demerara sugar.

3 In a large mixing bowl, whisk together the soft light brown sugar and caster sugar with the eggs until smooth and creamy and there are no lumps of sugar remaining. Add the yoghurt, vanilla and the rest of the melted butter and mix to combine.

4 In another bowl mash the bananas until very nearly smooth, add to the cake mixture and stir to combine. Sift the flour, baking powder, cinnamon and salt into the bowl, then add the chocolate chips and mix until everything is thoroughly combined.

5 Scoop the mixture into the prepared tin and spread to level it out. To decorate, slice the remaining banana in half lengthways and lay cut-side uppermost on top of the cake. Scatter with demerara sugar and bake on the middle shelf of the oven for 55–60 minutes until well risen and a skewer inserted into the middle of the cake comes out clean.

6 Leave the cake to cool in the tin for 3 minutes and then carefully lift it out onto a wire rack, peel off the baking paper and leave until cool.

Scrapper's devil's food cake

Scrapper is known as a daredevil: he creates the fireworks and light show for the Skeleton Squad and rides a motorcycle on stage. Scrapper also makes a mean devil's food cake and bakes one for the band at the start of every tour.

Makes 1 large cake (serves 10)

150g (5½oz) dark (bittersweet) chocolate, chopped

150g (5½oz) unsalted butter

325g (11½oz/2½ cups) plain (all-purpose) flour

25g (1oz/3½ tbsp) cocoa powder

1 tsp baking powder

2 tsp bicarbonate of soda (baking soda)

a pinch of salt

200g (7oz/generous 1 cup) soft light brown sugar

200g (7oz/1 cup) golden caster (superfine) sugar

4 medium eggs, lightly beaten

200g (7oz/scant 1 cup) soured cream

200ml (7fl oz/generous ¾ cup) boiling water

1 tsp vanilla extract or vanilla bean paste

1 Preheat the oven to (fan) 160°C/180°C/350°F/gas mark 4.

2 Melt the chocolate and the butter in a heatproof bowl either over a pan of barely simmering water (being careful to ensure the bottom of the bowl isn't touching the water) or in the microwave on a low setting. Stir until smooth, remove from the heat and leave to cool for 3–4 minutes.

3 Sift the flour, cocoa powder, baking powder, bicarbonate of soda and salt into a large mixing bowl. Add both sugars and use a balloon whisk to combine.

4 Make a well in the middle of the dry ingredients and add the beaten eggs, melted chocolate and butter, soured cream, boiling water and vanilla and whisk until smooth and thoroughly combined. Divide the mixture evenly between the cake tins, spread level and bake in the oven for about 25 minutes, until well risen and a skewer inserted into the middle of the cakes comes out clean.

5 Leave the cakes to cool in the tins for 15 minutes and then remove from the tins and leave on a wire rack until cold.

6 To make the frosting, melt the chocolate (in a bowl over a pan of simmering water or the microwave), stirring until smooth, then leave to cool slightly.

continued overleaf

Scrapper's devil's food cake
continued

For the frosting
150g (5½oz) dark
  (bittersweet) chocolate,
  chopped
250g (9oz) unsalted
  butter, softened
175g (6¼oz/1½ cups) icing
  (powdered) sugar, sifted
25g (1oz/3½ tbsp) cocoa
  powder, sifted
100g (3½oz) condensed milk
1 tsp vanilla extract or
  vanilla bean paste

To decorate
100g (3½oz) dark
  (bittersweet) chocolate,
  chopped

You will need:
balloon whisk
3 x 20cm (8in) round cake
  tins, base and sides
  greased and bases lined
  with baking paper
stand mixer

7 In a large mixing bowl or stand mixer fitted with the creamer attachment, beat the butter until pale, light and creamy and then gradually add the sifted icing sugar, scraping down the sides of the bowl from time to time. Add the cocoa powder, condensed milk and vanilla and mix until smooth. Add the cooled, melted chocolate and mix again until smooth.

8 Using a long, serrated knife, trim the tops of the cakes to make them level and place one of the cake layers on a serving plate. Spread 2–3 tablespoons of the frosting on top and sandwich with the second cake. Repeat and top with the third cake layer, gently pressing the layers together. Cover the top and sides of the cake with the remaining frosting, spreading it evenly with a palette knife to cover in generous swirls, then chill for 30 minutes to set.

9 To make the chocolate curls, melt the chocolate as instructed previously, stir until smooth and pour onto the underside of a flat baking sheet. Spread level to a thickness of about 3mm (⅛in). Sharply tap the baking sheet on the work surface to level the chocolate and to burst any air bubbles. Chill for 15 minutes until set but not solid.

10 Using a kitchen knife, hold the blade firmly at a 45-degree angle to the chocolate and push the blade across the top of the chocolate to create curls. Place the curls on a clean tray and chill until ready to use.

11 Cover the top of the cake with chocolate curls to serve.

STORAGE: Can be stored in an airtight box in the fridge for up to 2 days.

Cannon's caramel apple tarts

Cannon is a wellness coach who teaches kids how to make healthy meals. However, this candy corn can't resist a sweet treat during Halloween, so he makes his famous caramel apples for himself and all the trick or treaters!

Makes 6 tarts

For the caramelised apple purée
100g (3½oz/½ cup) caster (superfine) sugar, plus extra for sprinkling
25g (1oz) unsalted butter
a pinch of sea salt flakes
4 crisp eating apples, peeled, cored and quartered

For the tarts
plain (all-purpose) flour, for dusting
600g (1lb 5oz) puff pastry
6 crisp red-skinned apples
whole (full-fat) milk, for brushing
1 tbsp unsalted butter, melted
a sprinkling of golden caster (superfine) sugar
2 tbsp apricot jam
1 tsp lemon juice

You will need:
1 large baking sheet, lined with baking paper

1 First, prepare the caramelised apple purée. Tip the sugar into a small heavy-based frying pan (skillet), add 1 tablespoon of water and set the pan over a low heat to slowly melt the sugar. Continue to cook the sugar until it turns a rich, amber-coloured caramel, gently swirling the pan to ensure that it caramelises evenly. Add the butter and salt and stir to melt the butter and combine. Add the apples, stir to combine, cover the pan and cook over a low–medium heat for about 20 minutes, until the apples are super-soft. Remove the lid and cook off any excess syrup. Use the back of a spoon to mash the apples into a thick purée. Scoop into a bowl and leave to cool to room temperature while you make the tarts.

2 Dust a work surface with flour. Divide the pastry into 6 even pieces and roll each piece to a thickness of 2–3mm (⅛in). Using a 15cm (6in) plate as a guide, cut a disc from each piece of pastry and arrange on a large, lined baking sheet. Chill the pastry for 15 minutes while you preheat the oven to (fan) 180°C/200°C/400°F/gas mark 6.

3 Prepare the apples for the topping. Quarter and core the apples and cut each quarter into wafer-thin slices.

4 Brush a little milk around the top edge of each pastry disc and spoon a tablespoon of the caramelised apple purée into the middle and spread it to within 1cm (½in) of the edge. Neatly fan the sliced apples over the top of the apple purée and brush with melted butter. Sprinkle a little sugar over the apples and bake the tarts on the middle shelf of the oven for 15 minutes. Turn the tray around and bake for a further 15 minutes until the pastry is crisp and the apples are tender and starting to caramelize at the edges.

5 Melt the apricot jam with the lemon juice, strain to remove any lumps and brush over the top of the apples. Leave the tarts to cool to room temperature before serving.

STORAGE: Can be stored in an airtight box for up to 3 days.

Mac's pumpkin spiced whoopie pies

Meet Mac. He's decorating his treehouse for fall and Cornelias is helping him! They have snacks, and fabric samples to pick the perfect curtains. But Mac is having trouble deciding on the right shade of orange – pumpkin spice or pumpkin pie?

Makes 12 pies

125g (4½oz) unsalted butter
250g (9oz/1⅓ cups) dark muscovado sugar
2 medium eggs
200g (7oz) tinned pumpkin purée
2 tbsp soured cream
350g (12oz/2¾ cups) plain (all-purpose) flour
1 tsp baking powder
1 tsp bicarbonate of soda (baking soda)
2 tsp ground cinnamon
1 tsp mixed spice
1 tsp ground ginger
a pinch of salt

For the filling

125g (4½oz) unsalted butter, softened
100g (3½oz/scant ½ cup) cream cheese
125g (4½oz/scant 1¼ cups) icing (powdered) sugar, sifted, plus extra for dusting
4 tbsp maple syrup
1 tsp ground cinnamon
1 tsp vanilla extract or vanilla bean paste

You will need:

balloon whisk
2 baking sheets lined with baking paper
piping (pastry) bag fitted with a medium star nozzle

1 Preheat the oven to (fan) 150°C/170°C/325°F/gas mark 3.

2 Melt the butter in a pan or in a bowl in the microwave then leave it to cool slightly. In a large mixing bowl combine the sugar, eggs and pumpkin purée and mix with a balloon whisk until smooth. Add the melted butter and soured cream and mix again until combined.

3 Sift the flour, baking powder, bicarbonate of soda, spices and salt into the bowl and whisk until smooth and thoroughly combined.

4 Using an ice cream scoop or dessert spoon, place 12 scoops of batter on each lined baking sheet, leaving some space between each one to allow for spreading during cooking. Bake in the oven on the middle shelf for about 12 minutes until risen and the 'pies' spring back when pressed. Remove from the oven, leave to cool slightly then place on a wire rack to cool completely.

5 To make the filling, beat the butter until soft and smooth, add the cream cheese and mix until combined. Add the sifted icing sugar, maple syrup, cinnamon and vanilla and mix again until smooth. Spoon the filling into the piping bag fitted with a star nozzle.

6 Turn half of the whoopie pies over so that they are flat-side uppermost. Pipe a swirl of filling over the top of these pies and sandwich with the remaining pies. Dust the tops with icing sugar to serve.

STORAGE: Can be stored in an airtight box in the fridge for up to 2 days.

Veronica's pretzels

If you like adventure, pretzels, and crossing books off your reading list, Veronica is the octopus for you! With a book or two in each tentacle, you can be sure of some amazing adventures.

Makes 12 pretzels

500g (1lb 2oz/4 cups) strong white bread flour
2 tsp fast-action dried yeast
1 tsp salt
125ml (4fl oz/½ cup) warm water
125ml (4fl oz/½ cup) whole (full-fat) milk, warmed
50g (1¾oz) unsalted butter, softened
1 tbsp barley malt extract or molasses
1 medium egg, beaten with 1 tbsp milk to make a glaze
2–3 tsp sea salt flakes and/or white sesame seeds, to top

To cook
1 rounded tbsp bicarbonate of soda (baking soda)
2 tbsp soft light brown sugar
1 heaped tsp salt

You will need:
stand mixer
2 large baking sheets lined with baking paper

1 Tip the flour into the bowl of a stand mixer fitted with the dough hook, add the yeast and salt and mix to combine. Add the warm water, warm milk, softened butter and barley malt extract and knead for about 5 minutes until the dough is smooth and elastic.

2 Cover the bowl and leave at room temperature for 30 minutes to rest. Preheat the oven to (fan) 180°C/200°C/400°F/gas mark 6.

3 Turn the dough out of the bowl and knead for 10 seconds, then divide the dough into 12 even pieces. Using your hands, roll each ball into a neat rope roughly 45cm (18in) long. Shape the rope into a 'U', twist the ends twice and bring the ends back down to the bottom of the 'U' and press together to create a classic pretzel shape. Place on a lined baking sheet and repeat to make 12 pretzels.

4 Meanwhile, in a large saucepan, bring 2 litres (68fl oz) of water to the boil with the bicarbonate of soda, soft brown sugar and salt.

5 Gently lower the first 3 pretzels into the simmering water and cook gently for 30 seconds until they float to the surface and firm up slightly. Remove from the pan with a slotted spoon and return to the lined baking sheet. Poach all of the pretzels in the same way.

6 Brush the pretzels with the egg wash glaze, sprinkle with sea salt flakes or sesame seeds and bake in the oven for 12–15 minutes until golden brown and starting to crisp.

7 Remove from the oven and leave to cool on a wire rack.

STORAGE: Best eaten on the day of making.

Delilah's caramel, apple and blueberry muffins

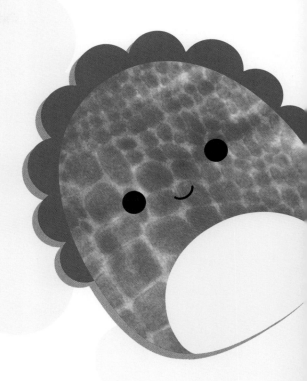

Delilah's favorite season is fall because she loves baking anything with apples! Apple donuts, apple muffins, and especially apple pie. Delilah is ready to jump into the kitchen. Do you want to be her baking assistant?

Makes 12 muffins

For the crumble topping
40g (1½oz/⅓ cup) plain (all-purpose) flour
40g (1½oz/¼ cup) demerara sugar
25g (1oz) unsalted butter, chilled and diced

For the muffins
1 large crisp eating apple
100g (3½oz) fresh blueberries
225g (8oz/1¾ cups) plain (all-purpose) flour, plus 2 tsp
2 tsp baking powder

1 Preheat the oven to (fan) 170°C/190°C/375°F/gas mark 5.

2 First, make the crumble topping. Tip all of the ingredients into a bowl and rub the butter into the dry ingredients using your fingertips until the mixture comes together in small clumps. Set aside while you prepare the muffin batter.

3 Peel, core and finely dice the apple. Tip most of the diced apple into a bowl, add the blueberries and the 2 teaspoons of flour and mix to combine. Save the remaining apple to sprinkle on top of the muffins.

4 Sift the 225g of flour, baking powder, bicarbonate of soda, cinnamon and salt into a large mixing bowl, then add the sugar.

5 In a jug whisk together the milk, soured cream, eggs and vanilla until combined.

6 Make a well in the middle of the dry ingredients, add the milk mixture and the melted butter and mix with a balloon whisk until only just

continued overleaf

Delilah's caramel, apple and blueberry muffins *continued*

½ tsp bicarbonate of soda
   (baking soda)
½ tsp ground cinnamon
a pinch of salt
175g (6¼oz/generous ¾ cup)
   caster (superfine) sugar
100ml (3½fl oz/scant ½ cup)
   whole (full-fat) milk
100ml (3½fl oz/scant ½ cup)
   soured cream or buttermilk
2 large eggs
1 tsp vanilla extract or
   vanilla bean paste
75g (2¾oz) unsalted
   butter, melted

To serve
12 tsp caramel sauce

You will need:
balloon whisk
12-hole muffin tin lined with
   large paper cases (or make
   your own using 15cm (6in)
   squares of baking paper)

combined (do not overmix – it's okay for the mixture to be a little lumpy at this stage). Fold the floury apples and blueberries into the batter using a large spoon.

7 Divide the batter evenly between the paper cases and scatter the top of each muffin with the remaining apple and the crumble topping.

8 Bake on the middle shelf of the oven for 25–30 minutes or until golden brown, well risen and a skewer inserted into the middle of a muffin comes out clean.

9 Serve warm or at room temperature, drizzled with caramel sauce.

STORAGE: Can be stored in an airtight box for up to 3 days.

Jason's mini coffee and walnut loaf cakes

Early mornings are hard for Jason, especially when he was up late studying! This donkey is studying to become a truck driver – he wants to drive trucks up through the mountains and beyond. Jason grew up loving trucks and can't wait to drive but only after he's had his coffee.

Makes 8 mini loaf cakes

150g (5½oz) unsalted butter, softened

100g (3½oz/½ cup) golden caster (superfine) sugar

50g (1¾oz/scant ¼ cup) soft light brown sugar

3 medium eggs, lightly beaten

3 tsp instant coffee powder

1 tsp cocoa powder

2 tsp boiling water

150g (5½oz/1¼ cups) plain (all-purpose) flour

1½ tsp baking powder

a pinch of salt

50g (1¾oz) walnuts, finely chopped

2 tbsp soured cream

1 Preheat the oven to (fan) 160°C/180°C/350°F/gas mark 4.

2 Cream the butter and both sugars together until the mixture is really pale and light. This is easiest using a stand mixer fitted with the creamer attachment and will take 3–4 minutes on medium speed.

3 Gradually add the beaten eggs, mixing well between each addition and scraping down the sides of the bowl from time to time with a rubber spatula. Dissolve the instant coffee and cocoa powder in the boiling water, add to the creamed mixture and mix to combine.

4 Sift the flour, baking powder and salt into the bowl, add the chopped walnuts and soured cream and fold into the cake mixture using a large metal spoon or rubber spatula until the mixture is smooth.

5 Divide the cake batter evenly between the mini loaf tins, spread level with a teaspoon and bake on the middle shelf of the oven for about 15 minutes until golden, well risen and a skewer inserted into the middle of the cakes comes out clean.

continued overleaf

Jason's mini coffee and walnut loaf cakes *continued*

For the coffee buttercream
3 tsp instant coffee powder
2 tsp boiling water
125g (4½oz) unsalted
   butter, softened
250g (9oz/2¼ cups) icing
   (powdered) sugar, sifted

To decorate
50g (1¾oz) walnut pieces
16 chocolate-coated coffee
   beans, roughly chopped
   (optional)

You will need:
stand mixer
8 mini loaf tins, greased and
   base and ends lined with
   a strip of baking paper
piping (pastry) bag fitted
   with a 1cm (½in) ribbon
   or leaf nozzle

6 Remove from the oven and leave the cakes to rest in the tin for 2 minutes, then turn out onto a wire rack and leave until cold.

7 To make the coffee buttercream, first dissolve the coffee in the boiling water. Beat the butter in a bowl until soft and light. Add the sifted icing sugar and coffee and beat again for about 1 minute until pale and light. Scoop the buttercream into the piping bag and generously cover the tops of the loaf cakes.

8 Scatter with walnut pieces and coffee beans (if using) to decorate.

STORAGE: Can be kept in an airtight box for up to 4 days.

Angie's peanut butter brownies

Angie adores a good fiesta – she loves going to parties and events as much as she enjoys hosting them. When Angie hosts, she makes specially themed food and drink for her friends. Want to know some of this Shiba Inu's favorite things to make? Guacamole, peanut butter brownies and samosas.

Makes 16–20 brownies

200g (7oz) dark (bittersweet) chocolate, chopped
175g (6¼oz) unsalted butter, diced
3 medium eggs
150g (5½oz/¾ cup) soft light brown sugar
100g (3½oz/½ cup) golden caster (superfine) sugar
1 tsp vanilla extract or vanilla bean paste
100g (3½oz/¾ cup) plain (all-purpose) flour
15g (½oz/2½ tbsp) cocoa powder
½ tsp baking powder
a good pinch of salt
150g (5½oz) peanut butter (crunchy or smooth)
100g (3½oz) mini peanut butter cups

You will need:
stand mixer or hand-held electric whisk
20 x 30cm (8 x 12in) brownie tin, greased and lined with baking paper
piping (pastry) bag

STORAGE: Will keep in an airtight box for up to 4 days.

1 Preheat the oven to (fan) 150°C/170°C/325°F/gas mark 3.

2 Tip the chopped chocolate and butter into a medium heatproof bowl and melt either over a pan of barely simmering water (being careful to ensure the bottom of the bowl isn't touching the water) or in the microwave on a low setting, stirring from time to time. Remove from the heat and leave to cool for 3–4 minutes.

3 Whisk the eggs, both sugars and the vanilla in a stand mixer on medium speed for about 3 minutes, until well aerated and paler in colour. Add the melted chocolate mixture and whisk again until just combined. Sift the flour, cocoa powder, baking powder and salt into the bowl and fold in using a rubber spatula until almost smooth.

4 Spoon the mixture into the prepared tin and spread level.

5 Warm the peanut butter until runny either in the microwave or in a heatproof bowl over a pan of simmering water. Spoon into a piping bag and drizzle over the top of the brownie mix (or use a spoon to drizzle). Using the tip of a knife, marble the peanut butter into the brownie mixture. Scatter the peanut butter cups evenly on top and bake on the middle shelf of the preheated oven for about 25 minutes, until the top is lightly risen and starting to crack.

6 Remove from the oven and leave to cool in the tin until completely cold before cutting into squares or rectangles to serve.

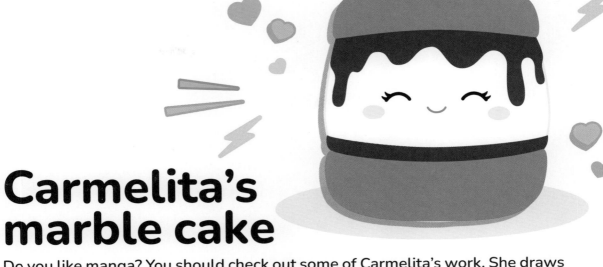

Carmelita's marble cake

Do you like manga? You should check out some of Carmelita's work. She draws black and white manga about school, her life, and adventures with her best friend Cinnamon. Don't worry about spilling any secrets: Carmelita uses code names for any juicy stuff.

**Makes 1 large cake
(serves 8–10)**

90g (3oz) dark (bittersweet)
   chocolate, chopped
225g (8oz) unsalted
   butter, softened
225g (8oz/1⅛ cups) caster
   (superfine) sugar
2 tsp vanilla extract or
   vanilla bean paste
4 medium eggs, lightly
   beaten
225g (8oz/1¾ cups) plain
   (all-purpose) flour
25g (1oz) cornflour
   (cornstarch)
3 tsp baking powder
a pinch of salt
50g (1¾oz/scant ½ cup)
   ground almonds
   (almond meal)
3 tbsp whole (full-fat) milk
2 tsp cocoa powder
1 tbsp hot water

1 Preheat the oven to (fan) 150°C/170°C/325°F/gas mark 3.

2 To make the cake, first tip the dark chocolate into a heatproof bowl and melt either over a pan of barely simmering water (being careful to ensure the bottom of the bowl isn't touching the water) or in the microwave on a low setting, stirring from time to time.

3 In the bowl of a stand mixer fitted with the creamer attachment, cream the softened butter with the sugar and vanilla for 2–3 minutes until pale and light.

4 Scrape down the sides of the bowl with a rubber spatula then gradually add the beaten eggs, mixing well between each addition.

5 Sift the flour, cornflour, baking powder and salt into the bowl. Add the ground almonds and milk and mix until smooth. In a small bowl combine the cocoa powder and hot water and mix until smooth.

6 Scoop half of the cake mixture into another bowl, then add the melted chocolate and cocoa paste and beat until smooth and thoroughly combined.

7 Using two tablespoons, dollop alternate spoonfuls of chocolate and vanilla cake mixture into the prepared tin until all the mixture has been used up and the tin is roughly two-thirds full. Tap the bottom of the

continued overleaf

Carmelita's marble cake

continued

For the chocolate fudge frosting

100g (3½oz) dark (bittersweet) chocolate, chopped
100g (3½oz) milk chocolate, chopped
25g (1oz) unsalted butter
4 tbsp double (heavy) cream
2 tbsp golden syrup (light treacle)

To decorate

175g (6¼oz) chocolate-coated honeycomb balls
100g (3½oz) white chocolate drops

You will need:

stand mixer
1 x 900g (2lb) loaf tin (base, ends and sides greased and lined with baking paper)

tin sharply on the work surface to level it, then drag a round-bladed knife or the handle of a wooden spoon 4 or 5 times through the batter to lightly swirl the chocolate and vanilla cake mixes together.

8 Bake on the middle shelf of the oven for 50 minutes to 1 hour until well risen, golden brown and a skewer inserted into the middle of the cake comes out clean.

9 Leave the cake to cool in the tin for 10 minutes and then turn out onto a wire rack and leave until completely cold before frosting.

10 To prepare the frosting, tip both the dark and milk chocolate into a heatproof bowl and melt either over a pan of simmering water (being careful to ensure the bottom of the bowl isn't touching the water) or in the microwave on a low setting, stirring from time to time. Add the butter, cream and golden syrup and mix to combine. Leave to cool and thicken for 30 minutes and then spoon the frosting over the top of the cooled cake.

11 Decorate with chocolate honeycomb balls and white chocolate drops and leave to set for a further 20 minutes before cutting and serving.

STORAGE: Store in an airtight box for up to 4 days.

Hans's chocolate truffles

Hans the Hedgehog has seen every movie ever and loves to eat pudding, especially with sprinkles. Actually, when it comes to food, he's willing to try whatever someone puts on his plate, probably because he is so open to change and adventure.

Makes 25–30 truffles

200ml (7fl oz/generous ¾ cup) double (heavy) cream
2 tbsp brandy or dark rum (or the same volume of orange juice)
25g (1oz/2 tbsp) light muscovado sugar
1 tsp vanilla extract or vanilla bean paste
finely grated zest of ½ orange, unwaxed
a pinch of salt
250g (9oz) dark (bittersweet) chocolate, finely chopped

To coat
100g (3½oz) dark (bittersweet) chocolate, chopped
assorted sugar sprinkles

1 Pour the cream and brandy (or rum or orange juice) into a small saucepan, add the sugar, vanilla, orange zest and salt and heat gently until the cream is hot but not boiling.

2 Tip the finely chopped chocolate into a mixing bowl, then pour the hot cream mixture over the top. Leave for 1 minute, then gently stir until smooth. Leave to cool and then cover and chill for at least 2 hours or until you have a firm ganache.

3 Using your hands and a teaspoon, roll the ganache into 25–30 cherry-sized balls, arrange on a baking paper-covered tray and chill again for 15 minutes while you melt the remaining 100g (3½oz) chocolate for the coating. Tip the chopped chocolate into a medium heatproof bowl and melt either over a pan of simmering water (being careful to ensure the bottom of the bowl isn't touching the water) or in the microwave on a low setting, stirring from time to time.

4 Tip the sugar sprinkles onto plates. Drop one truffle at a time into the melted chocolate to coat, then remove with a fork, allowing the excess chocolate to drip back into the bowl. Return the chocolate-coated truffles to a clean, baking paper-lined tray and leave for 30 seconds before rolling in the sugar sprinkles to coat.

5 Repeat with the remaining truffles and leave to set firm before serving.

STORAGE: Store truffles in an airtight box in the fridge for up to 1 week and bring to room temperature to serve.

Zuzana's triple choc chip cookies

Zuzana plays the guitar and has a big tour coming up. She can't live without extra rhinestones and a big box of her mom's chocolate chip cookies, she can't go without them!

Makes 20–22 cookies

75g (2¾oz) dark (bittersweet) chocolate, chopped

200g (7oz) white chocolate

200g (7oz) unsalted butter, softened

125g (4½oz/⅔ cup) soft light brown sugar

75g (2¾oz/⅓ cup) caster (superfine) sugar

2 medium eggs, lightly beaten

1 tsp vanilla extract or vanilla bean paste

225g (8oz/1¾ cups) plain (all-purpose) flour

25g (1oz/3½ tbsp) cocoa powder

1 tsp bicarbonate of soda (baking soda)

a good pinch of salt

2 tbsp whole (full-fat) milk

100g (3½oz) dark (bittersweet) chocolate chips

1 Melt the 75g (2¾oz) dark chocolate in a heatproof bowl either over a pan of barely simmering water (being careful to ensure the bottom of the bowl isn't touching the water) or in the microwave on a low setting, stirring from time to time. Remove from the heat and leave to cool slightly.

2 Chop the white chocolate into 1cm (½in) pieces and set aside.

3 In a stand mixer fitted with the creamer attachment, beat the softened butter with both sugars for about 1 minute until smooth and combined but not until fluffy. Gradually add the beaten eggs, mixing well and scraping down the sides of the bowl with a spatula between each addition. Add the vanilla and mix again.

4 Scoop the melted chocolate into the mixture and mix until combined. Scrape down the sides of the bowl with a rubber spatula, sift the flour, cocoa powder, bicarbonate of soda and salt into the bowl. Add the milk and mix again until thoroughly combined.

5 Fold two thirds of the white chocolate and all of the dark chocolate chips into the cookie mixture. Using two dessert spoons, shape the mixture into 20–22 rough-shaped but even-sized balls and place on a lined baking sheet. Press the remaining white chocolate into the cookie dough balls. Cover and chill for 1 hour until firm and then once again roll each cookie ball in your hands into a smooth, firm ball. Cover and chill again for 4 hours or overnight.

continued overleaf

Zuzana's triple choc chip cookies
continued

You will need:
stand mixer
2 large baking sheets lined
   with baking paper
1 x 10cm (4in) round cutter

6 Preheat the oven to (fan) 150°C/170°C/325°F/gas mark 3.

7 Place 6–8 dough balls on each lined baking sheet, allowing plenty of space between each one for spreading during cooking. Bake in the oven for 10 minutes then remove from the oven and bang the bottom of the sheet on the work surface to deflate the cookies a little. Place the cutter around the cookies while they're still on the baking sheet and swirl it round and round to make neat round cookies. Return the cookies to the oven for a further 2–4 minutes until firm but not crisp. The cookies will firm up further on cooling.

8 Continue baking the cookies in batches. Leave to cool on the baking sheets until firm and then transfer to a wire rack until cold.

STORAGE: Store in airtight boxes between layers of baking paper for up to 4 days.

Caden's s'mores

Caden can pitch a tent in a snap! She goes camping every year and knows all the tricks to make it easy and fun. This 'Mallow always has a compass and first aid kit handy, and they never forget to pack chocolate bars for nightly s'mores parties. Join Caden on their next big camping trip!

Makes 12 sandwiches

1 quantity of squishmallows 'mallows (see page 127)

For the biscuits
125g (4½oz) unsalted butter, softened
50g (1¾oz) soft light brown sugar
1 tbsp golden syrup (light treacle)
150g (5½oz/1¼ cups) plain (all-purpose) flour, plus extra for dusting
¼ tsp baking powder
¼ tsp bicarbonate of soda (baking soda)
1 tsp mixed spice
a pinch of salt
25g (1oz) oat bran or ground almonds (almond meal)
100g (3½oz) dark (bittersweet) chocolate, chopped
½ tsp sunflower oil
edible sprinkles
12 tsp Biscoff spread

You will need:
5cm (2in) round cutter

1 Make the marshmallow mixture following the recipe on page 127.

2 While you wait for the marshmallow to set, make the biscuits. Using a wooden spoon, cream together the softened butter and brown sugar until pale and light. Add the golden syrup and mix to combine. Sift the dry ingredients into the bowl, stir in the oat bran or ground almonds, and use a rubber spatula or wooden spoon to mix until the dough comes together into a smooth ball. Flatten into a disc, wrap in cling film (plastic wrap) and chill for about 1 hour until firm.

3 Lightly dust a work surface with flour and roll the dough out to a thickness of about 3mm (⅛in). Use a cutter to stamp out rounds from the dough and arrange on lined baking sheets. Gather up the scraps and roll out and stamp out more biscuits – you want 24 biscuits in total. Chill for 20 minutes.

4 Preheat the oven to (fan) 160°C/180°C/350°F/gas mark 4.

5 Bake the biscuits in the oven for about 10 minutes until crisp. Remove from the oven and leave to cool on the baking sheets.

6 Tip the chopped chocolate into a medium heatproof bowl, add the sunflower oil, and melt either over a pan of simmering water (being careful to ensure the bottom of the bowl isn't touching the water) or in the microwave on a low setting, stirring from time to time.

7 Dip half of each biscuit in the melted chocolate. Scatter the chocolate with sprinkles and leave to set, sprinkle side up.

8 Using the cutter, stamp out discs from the marshmallow and lightly toast either with a kitchen blowtorch or on sticks over a fire. Spread the underside of half of the biscuits with a teaspoon of Biscoff spread, place a toasted marshmallow on top, sandwich with another biscuit and eat while the marshmallow is still warm and the chocolate is starting to melt.

STORAGE: Best eaten on the day of making.

Caedyn's apple and raspberry pie

Do you like apple pies and movie nights? So does Caedyn! She loves baking pies and watching scary movies, especially for a movie marathon. She loves a monster movie with a side of fresh pie. Would you like to join her?

Serves 8

For the pastry

400g (14oz/3¼ cups) plain (all-purpose) flour, plus extra for dusting

a good pinch of salt

250g (9oz) unsalted butter, chilled and diced, plus extra for greasing

3 tbsp golden caster (superfine) sugar, plus a little extra for sprinkling

2 medium egg yolks (save 1 white for glazing)

2 tsp lemon juice

3 tbsp ice-cold water

a little milk, for brushing

For the filling

1kg (2¼lb) apples – an equal mix of tart, crisp apples and sweet apples such as Braeburns

1 Start by making the pastry. Tip the flour into a large bowl and add the salt. Add the chilled, diced butter and rub it in using your fingertips until there are only a few small pieces of butter remaining and the mixture resembles breadcrumbs. Stir in the sugar. Make a well in the middle, add the egg yolks, lemon juice and ice-cold water and mix again, using a palette knife to bring the dough together. Tip the dough out of the bowl onto the work surface, knead very briefly, divide in half, shape each piece into a ball and flatten into two discs. Cover and chill for 1 hour or until firm.

2 Dust a work surface with flour, then unwrap and roll one piece of dough into a neat disc that is larger than the pie dish by about 5cm (2in) all round. Grease the pie dish, then carefully line with the pastry, allowing excess to hang over the edges.

3 Start on the filling: peel, core and thinly slice the apples and tip the slices into a large bowl. Add the raspberries, sugar, cornflour and lemon juice and mix well to combine. Scoop the mixture into the pastry-lined pie dish.

4 Unwrap the remaining pastry and roll it out into a neat disc with a diameter at least 5cm (2in) wider than the top of the pie dish. Cut the pastry into neat 2cm (¾in)-wide strips.

continued overleaf

Caedyn's apple and raspberry pie *continued*

225g (8oz) raspberries
3 tbsp golden caster (superfine) sugar, plus extra for sprinkling
1 tbsp cornflour (cornstarch)
juice of ½ lemon

To serve
crème fraîche or vanilla ice cream

You will need:
metal pie dish with a base measurement of 20cm (8in)

STORAGE: Best eaten on the day of making, but will keep in a covered container in the fridge.

5 Lattice the pastry strips across the top of the pie. Make sure that you keep the lattice even and neat, with the strips lying close together. When the whole of the pie is covered, use a sharp knife to trim off any excess pastry from the edges. Brush the edge of the pie with milk, press the lattice strips to seal and use your fingers to crimp the edges decoratively.

6 Chill the pie for 30 minutes while you preheat the oven to (fan) 170°C/190°C/375°F/gas mark 5 and place a baking tray on the middle shelf to heat up at the same time.

7 Lightly beat the egg white, then brush it over the top of the pie, scatter with around 1 tablespoon of sugar and cook on the hot baking tray for 30 minutes. Turn the pie around, reduce the oven temperature to (fan) 150°C /170°C/325°F/gas mark 3 and continue to cook for a further 25–30 minutes until the pastry is a good, deep golden brown and the apples are bubbling and tender when tested with a skewer.

8 Leave to cool slightly and then serve with crème fraîche or vanilla ice cream.

Manny's gingerbread houses

Manny is quite the handyman. He enjoys picking up the pieces. He's known for building the most memorable gingerbread houses every year. He hopes to connect creativity and machines as an engineer in the future.

Makes 8–12 houses

2 tbsp golden syrup (light treacle)
1 medium egg yolk
200g (7oz/1⅔ cups) plain (all-purpose) flour, plus extra for dusting
½ tsp baking powder
2 tsp ground ginger
1 tsp ground cinnamon
1 tsp mixed spice
a pinch of salt
100g (3½oz) unsalted butter, chilled and diced
75g (2¾oz/⅓ cup) light muscovado sugar

To decorate

500g (1lb 2oz) icing (powdered) sugar
orange food colouring paste

You will need:

2 baking sheets lined with baking paper
2 small disposable piping (pastry) bags

1 Mix together the golden syrup and egg yolk in a small bowl. In a separate, large bowl, sift the flour, baking powder, spices and salt and add the butter. Rub the butter into the flour using your fingers but trying not to overwork the mixture. When the mixture resembles fine sand and there are only very small flecks of butter remaining, add the muscovado sugar and mix again to incorporate. Add the golden syrup and egg yolk mixture and mix again until the dough starts to clump together. Use your hands to gently knead the dough into a smooth ball. Flatten the dough into a disc, wrap in cling film (plastic wrap) and chill for 1 hour.

2 Meanwhile, draw assorted house shapes on baking paper and cut them out to use as templates. These can vary in size from about 8–12cm (3–4¾in).

3 Lightly dust the work surface with flour and roll the dough out to a thickness of about 3mm (⅛in). Lay the templates on the gingerbread and cut out gingerbread houses using a small sharp knife. Carefully arrange on the lined baking sheets, leaving a little space between each house.

4 Gather any dough scraps together, knead gently into a ball and re-roll and cut out more houses. Chill the unbaked biscuits for 20 minutes while you preheat the oven to (fan) 160°C/180°C/350°F/gas mark 4.

5 Bake the gingerbread houses on the middle shelf of the oven for about 12 minutes until firm and just starting to brown slightly at the edges. Remove from the oven and leave to cool on the baking sheets.

continued overleaf

6 Sift the icing sugar into a bowl and add cold water a teaspoon at a time, whisking constantly until the icing holds a firm ribbon trail when the whisk is lifted from the bowl. Spoon 1 tablespoon of the icing into another bowl and tint orange using a tiny dot of the food colouring paste. Scoop the orange icing into a piping bag, snip the end into a fine writing point, twist the opening to seal, cover with a tea towel and set aside.

7 Spoon the remaining icing into another piping bag, snip the end into a fine writing point and twist the opening end to seal the icing in.

8 Pipe decorative lines, roof tiles, windows and doors over each gingerbread house with the white icing. Embellish each house with orange icing and leave to set for about 1 hour before serving.

STORAGE: Will keep for up to 1 week in an airtight box.

SQUAD

Baking extras

Squishmallows marshmallows

sunflower oil, for greasing
1 tbsp icing (powdered)
   sugar
1 tbsp cornflour (cornstarch)
6 leaves platinum-grade
   leaf gelatine
2 large egg whites
a pinch of salt
350g (12oz/1¾ cups) caster
   (superfine) sugar
1 tbsp liquid glucose or
   golden syrup (light treacle)
1 tsp vanilla extract or
   vanilla bean paste

You will need:
stand mixer
20 x 30cm (8 x 12in)
   baking tin
sugar thermometer

1 Lightly grease the baking tin with sunflower oil, line with cling film (plastic wrap) or baking paper and lightly grease the film or paper.

2 Mix the icing sugar and cornflour together in a small bowl and dust a small amount over the lined tin in an even coating. Set the remaining sugar mix aside.

3 Soak the gelatine leaves in a bowl of cold water for about 10 minutes until soft. Place the egg whites in the bowl of a stand mixer fitted with the whisk attachment, add the salt and 1 tablespoon of the caster sugar but do not start mixing just yet.

4 Tip the remaining caster sugar and liquid glucose (or golden syrup) into a medium saucepan and add 150ml (5fl oz/⅔ cup) water. Place the pan over a medium heat and stir to dissolve the sugar. Bring to the boil and continue to cook until the syrup reaches 120°C/248°F on the sugar thermometer. Slide the pan off the heat.

5 Working quickly, drain the softened gelatine and pat dry on kitchen paper. Whisk the egg whites until they hold stiff peaks. Add the gelatine to the hot syrup and stir until completely melted. With the motor running on slow–medium speed, add the hot syrup to the whisked egg whites in a steady stream. Add the vanilla and continue to whisk for about 5 minutes until the mixture is cool, very glossy white and stiff enough to hold a firm ribbon trail when the whisk is lifted from the bowl.

6 Scoop the marshmallow mixture into the prepared tin and spread level with a palette knife. Leave to set in a cool place for at least 2 hours, then dust the top with the remaining icing sugar mixture, cover with cling film and leave for another 4 hours or overnight.

Ultimate buttercreams

Regular buttercream

Makes enough for 12 cupcakes

100g (3½oz) unsalted
 butter, softened
200g (7oz/1¾ cups) icing
 (powdered) sugar, sifted

1 Using a wooden spoon or rubber spatula,
cream together the butter and icing sugar
in a bowl until really pale and light.

2 Scoop the buttercream into a piping bag.

Meringue buttercream

Makes enough for 12 cupcakes

4 medium egg whites
225g (8oz/1⅛ cups) caster
 (superfine) sugar
a pinch of salt
360g (12¾oz) unsalted
 butter, softened
2 tsp vanilla extract or
 vanilla bean paste

1 Using a balloon whisk, combine the egg
whites, sugar and salt in a large heatproof
bowl. Set the bowl over a pan of gently
simmering water and whisk continuously
for about 5 minutes until the meringue
is glossy white, hot to the touch and thick
enough to hold a ribbon trail when the
whisk is lifted from the bowl.

2 Scoop the meringue into the bowl
of a stand mixer fitted with the whisk
attachment and whisk on medium speed
for about 5 minutes until stiff, glossy and
cold. Scrape down the sides of the mixer
bowl using a rubber spatula.

3 Gradually add the softened butter to the
cold meringue mixture, whisking continuously
and scraping down the sides of the bowl
from time to time. When all the butter has
been added the frosting should be silky
smooth, thick and glossy. Add the vanilla
and mix again to combine.

4 Spoon the buttercream neatly into
a piping (pastry) bag.

Caramel sauce

This sauce can be used to pour over cakes, pancakes, ice cream, banana split, baked apples... Or simply eaten with a spoon!

75g (2¾oz/⅓ cup) dark muscovado sugar

75g (2¾oz/⅓ cup) golden syrup (light treacle)

150ml (5fl oz/⅔ cup) double (heavy) cream

50g (1¾oz) unsalted butter

125g (4½oz) caster (superfine) sugar

1 tsp vanilla extract or vanilla bean paste

a good pinch of sea salt flakes

1 Measure the muscovado sugar, golden syrup, double cream and butter into a small pan and set over a low heat to melt the butter and dissolve the sugar. Bring to the boil, remove from the heat and keep warm.

2 Tip the caster sugar into a medium-sized, solid-bottomed saucepan and add 2 tablespoons of water. It is important not to use a small pan here as the caramel will bubble up quite furiously as it cooks. Set the pan over a low–medium flame and heat without stirring until the sugar has dissolved. Swirl the pan to dissolve the sugar and if any sugar crystals form on the side of the pan, brush the insides of the pan with a clean pastry brush dipped in water. Once all of the sugar has dissolved, bring the syrup to the boil and continue to cook steadily and without stirring until it becomes a rich amber colour. Slide the pan off the heat and carefully and slowly add the warm cream and sugar mixture.

3 Stir to combine then return the pan to a low heat and simmer for a further 30 seconds. Add the vanilla and salt and set aside to cool.

129

Drinks

Bowie's watermelon fresca

Bowie is one sleepy hedgehog, but she only likes to sleep because she has such big dreams! Bowie is an entrepreneur and one day plans on bringing fascinating innovations to the whole 'Mallow world, just after she wakes up from this nap...

Serves 4

650g (1lb 7oz) skinned and diced watermelon, pips removed
juice of 1 lime
3–4 tbsp caster (superfine) sugar
350ml (12fl oz/1½ cups) sparkling water
ice cubes, to serve
mint sprigs, to garnish
lime slices, to garnish
lime and chilli seasoning (optional)

You will need:
blender
fine-mesh sieve

1 Tip the diced watermelon into a blender and whizz until completely smooth. Add the lime juice and 3 tablespoons of the sugar and blend again to combine. If the fresca is not completely smooth, strain it into a jug through a fine-mesh sieve.

2 Add the sparkling water, taste and add a little more sugar or lime juice to taste.

3 Pour into ice-filled glasses and garnish each glass with a sprig of mint and slice of lime and perhaps a sprinkle of lime and chilli seasoning if you like things a little spicy!

Danielle's strawberry and kiwi smoothie

Meet Danielle. She loves playing music, video games, and strawberry kiwi smoothies. Danielle plays the piano and is learning how to play the music from her favorite video games for her next recital. What song would you like her to play?

Serves 3–4

250g (9oz) strawberries, plus extra slices to garnish
2 kiwi fruit, plus extra slices to garnish
1 ripe banana
200g (7oz/scant 1 cup) natural yoghurt
6–8 ice cubes

You will need:
blender

1 Remove the green leafy tops from the strawberries and peel and roughly chop the kiwi. Peel and roughly slice the banana.

2 Tip all of the fruit into a blender, add the yoghurt and ice cubes and blend until smooth.

3 Pour into glasses and garnish with sliced strawberries and kiwi.

133

Mony's raspberry lemonade

Meet Mony. She loves adventures and fruity drinks! Mony and her friends migrate south every year for a tropical vacation. She always packs extra sunscreen, her favorite striped swimsuit, and an interesting book to read on the beach! Want to join this year?

Serves 6

250g (9oz/1¼ cups) caster (superfine) sugar
juice of 5 lemons
200g (7oz) raspberries, fresh or frozen, plus extra to garnish
1 litre (34fl oz/4 cups) sparkling water
ice cubes, to serve
lemon slices, to garnish

You will need:
blender
fine-mesh sieve

1 Tip the sugar into a small saucepan, add 250ml (8½fl oz/1 cup) water and bring to the boil, stirring to dissolve the sugar. Remove from the heat and leave to cool to room temperature.

2 Add the lemon juice to the sugar syrup.

3 Tip the raspberries into a blender with 4 tablespoons of the lemon syrup and blend until smooth. Push the raspberry mixture through a fine-mesh sieve to remove any pips and add the purée to the rest of the lemon syrup. Mix well to combine and pour into a large jug.

4 Add the sparkling water and mix well to combine.

5 Pour into ice-filled glasses and garnish with lemon slices and extra raspberries.

134

Gigi's apple spritz

This 'Mallow moves a mile a minute, thanks to her favorite fuel: apple juice! When Gigi is around, you are sure to smell a hint of apple before you see her. How many is too many? The limit does not exist!

Serves 8

10 raspberries, plus extra to garnish
3 tbsp elderflower cordial
500ml (18fl oz/2 cups) cloudy apple juice
1 litre (34fl oz/4 cups) sparkling, soda or tonic water
ice cubes, to serve
1 apple, thinly sliced, to garnish

You will need:
fine-mesh sieve

1 Crush the raspberries in a small bowl using a fork, add the elderflower cordial and mix to combine. Strain through a fine-mesh sieve into a jug, pushing down on the fruit to extract all of the juice but not the raspberry seeds. Add the apple juice and mix to combine.

2 Pour into a large jug, add the sparkling, soda or tonic water and mix to combine.

3 Fill tall glasses with ice cubes and apple slices, pour over the spritz and garnish with raspberries.

135

Luanne's iced tea

Luanne loves long summer nights on her front porch. She sits in her rocking chair and keeps a wooden folding fan handy in case the air gets too humid. Luanne made a pitcher of iced tea this afternoon. Will you come over and share a glass with Luanne?

Serves 4

4 tea bags
3–4 tbsp golden caster (superfine) sugar, plus extra if needed
1 unwaxed lemon, thinly sliced
ice cubes, to serve
1 ripe peach, sliced, to garnish
4 fresh mint sprigs, to garnish

1 Bring 500ml (18fl oz/2 cups) of water to the boil and pour into a heatproof jug. Add the tea bags and leave to brew for 20 minutes.

2 Remove the tea bags and add the sugar and a further 500ml (18fl oz/2 cups) of cold water and mix until combined and the sugar has dissolved.

3 Add the thinly sliced lemon to the tea, cover and chill for 1 hour. Taste and add more sugar if needed.

4 Serve in tall glasses with plenty of ice cubes and garnish with peach slices and sprigs of mint.

Starla's instant berry slushie

Meet Starla. She loves fruity iced teas, board games, and exploration. Starla is an ocean studies major and wants to keep the ocean clean and safe for everyone. Her parents raised her to care about environmental issues and inspired her to study how to keep the sea safe for all creatures!

Serves 2

2 tbsp caster (superfine) sugar
200g (7oz) frozen berry mix
250ml (8½fl oz/1 cup) cranberry juice
300g (10½oz) ice cubes
1 small punnet of fresh berries, to garnish (blackberries, strawberries, raspberries, etc.)

You will need:
blender

1 To make a quick sugar syrup, put the sugar in a small saucepan with 1 tablespoon of water and bring to a gentle simmer over a low-medium heat. Once simmering, remove from the heat and allow the syrup to cool for a couple of minutes until the sugar has fully dissolved.

2 Add the frozen berries, cranberry juice and sugar syrup to a blender and blitz until smooth.

3 Wrap the ice cubes in a clean tea towel and bash them with a rolling pin to crush them into small pieces. Add the crushed ice to the blender with the berry mix and pulse until you have a smooth slushie consistency (if you are using a small blender, you may need to do this in 2 batches). If the slushie is lumpy you may need to muddle it with a wooden spoon a few times between pulses.

4 Divide between 2 glasses and garnish each with a small handful of fresh berries.

Fabi's pumpkin spiced latte

Meet fabulous Fabi! Fabi loves pumpkin-flavored treats and hiding in plain sight. She can camouflage herself in most surroundings, which is helpful when Fabi wants to curl up and take a long nap. Keep a pumpkin latte on hand when you're on the lookout for Fabi!

Serves 2

300ml (10½fl oz/1¼ cups) milk of your choice
2 tbsp tinned pumpkin purée
¼ tsp ground cinnamon, plus extra for sprinkling
¼ tsp freshly grated nutmeg, plus extra for sprinkling
¼ tsp ground ginger
1 star anise
1 tsp vanilla extract
1–2 tsp caster (superfine) sugar
90ml (3fl oz/⅓ cup) freshly brewed, strong coffee
4 tbsp whipped cream, to serve (optional)

1 Put the milk, pumpkin purée, spices, vanilla extract and sugar in a small saucepan and whisk over a low heat until very gently simmering. Once the milk starts to simmer, remove from the heat.

2 Remove the whole star anise. And if you have a milk frother, we recommend frothing the pumpkin-spiced milk at this stage.

3 Serve the coffee in 2 mugs or heatproof glasses and pour over the hot pumpkin-spiced milk. Finish with whipped cream (if using) and an extra dusting of cinnamon and/or nutmeg.

Puff's hot chocolate with all the trimmings

Puff loves melting cheese in his hot cocoa and sharing smiles with friends. He can also be a bit silly sometimes. But did you know, Puff is great at keeping secrets too! Wanna share some laughs with Puff?

Serves 2

150g (5½oz) 70% dark (bittersweet) chocolate, chopped

50g (1¾oz) milk chocolate, chopped

350ml (12fl oz/1½ cups) whole (full-fat) milk

200ml (7fl oz/generous ¾ cup) double (heavy) cream

1 cinnamon stick

2–3 tbsp maple syrup

1 tsp vanilla extract or vanilla bean paste

a pinch of salt

1 tsp cocoa powder, to serve

3 tbsp mini marshmallows, to serve

You will need:

hand-held electric whisk

1 Place both types of chopped chocolate in a heatproof mixing bowl or jug.

2 Combine the milk and half of the double cream in a medium saucepan. Add the cinnamon stick, maple syrup, vanilla and salt. Slowly bring to the boil over a low heat to allow the cinnamon to infuse the milk and cream.

3 Pour the hot milk mixture over the chopped chocolate and whisk until smooth. Return the mixture to the pan and gently reheat over a low flame, whisking constantly, until just below boiling point. Pour into mugs or heatproof glasses.

4 Whip the remaining cream with a hand-held electric whisk until it holds stiff peaks and spoon some on top of each serving.

5 Dust with cocoa powder, scatter with mini marshmallows and serve immediately.

Conversions

G/OZ

5g (⅛oz)

7g (¼oz)

15g (½oz)

20g (¾oz)

25g (1oz)

30g (1¼oz)

35g (1¼oz)

40g (1½oz)

50g (1¾oz)

65g (2oz)

75g (2¾oz)

85g (3oz)

100g (3½oz)

115g (4oz)

125g (4½oz)

150g (5½oz)

175g (6¼oz)

200g (7oz)

225g (8oz)

250g (9oz)

275g (9¾oz)

300g (10½oz)

350g (12oz)

400g (14oz)

450g (1lb)

500g (1lb 2oz)

550g (1lb 3½oz)

600g (1lb 5oz)

650g (1lb 7oz)

1kg (2¼lb)

ML/FL OZ

50ml (1¾fl oz/3½ tbsp)

100ml (3½fl oz/scant ½ cup)

120ml (4fl oz/½ cup)

125ml (4fl oz/½ cup)

150ml (5fl oz/⅔ cup)

200ml (7fl oz/generous ¾ cup)

225ml (7½fl oz/scant 1 cup)

250ml (8½fl oz/1 cup)

325ml (11fl oz/1⅜ cups)

350ml (12fl oz/1½ cups)

400ml (13½fl oz/1⅔ cups)

500ml (18fl oz/2 cups)

1 litre (34fl oz/4 cups)

CM/IN

3mm (⅛in)

5mm (¼in)

1cm (½in)

2cm (¾in)

3cm (1¼in)

5cm (2in)

6cm (2½in)

7cm (2¾in)

8cm (3in)

10cm (4in)

12cm (4¾in)

15cm (6in)

18cm (7in)

20cm (8in)

23cm (9in)

30cm (12in)

33cm (13in)

40cm (16in)

45cm (18in)

50cm (20in)

Index

Quarto

First published in 2024 by White Lion Publishing,
an imprint of The Quarto Group.

1 Triptych Place
London, SE1 9SH
United Kingdom
T (0)20 7700 6700
www.quarto.com

A catalogue record for this book is available
from the British Library.

ISBN 978-0-7112-9330-4
eBook ISBN 978-1-83600-175-1

10 9 8 7 6 5 4 3 2 1

Art Director and Designer: Smith & Gilmour
Food Photography: Smith & Gilmour
Recipe Developer, Writer and Food Stylist: Annie Rigg
Publisher: Jessica Axe
Production Controller: Rohana Yusof

Printed in China